Agnes M. Stewart

Life in the cloister

Or, faithful and true

Agnes M. Stewart

Life in the cloister
Or, faithful and true

ISBN/EAN: 9783741178061

Manufactured in Europe, USA, Canada, Australia, Japa

Cover: Foto ©Lupo / pixelio.de

Manufactured and distributed by brebook publishing software (www.brebook.com)

Agnes M. Stewart

Life in the cloister

Life in the Cloister;

OR,

FAITHFUL AND TRUE.

Treu und Fest.

BY THE AUTHOR OF "THE WORLD AND THE CLOISTER,"
&c., &c., &c.

"Look on this picture, and on this."—*Hamlet.*

BALTIMORE:
PUBLISHED BY KELLY & PIET,
174 Baltimore Street.

To

The Saintly and Virtuous,
but
Much Maligned and Calumniated,

Religious in the Conventual Establishments of

GREAT BRITAIN AND IRELAND,

𝔗𝔥𝔦𝔰 𝔏𝔦𝔱𝔱𝔩𝔢 𝔅𝔬𝔬𝔨

Is affectionately inscribed by the Authoress,
a faint tribute of respect and esteem for their many
Virtues, and the sublimity and self-denial
of that
HIDDEN and INTERIOR Life of the Cloister,
ich those of the Catholic Faith can alone appreciate,
but which the falsely-judging world so utterly
ignores, and, in its ignorance, condemns.

Preface.

ON placing this little volume before the public, we feel ourselves called upon to advert to a mischievous work recently published, entitled "Memoirs of Henrietta Caracciolo," an ex-Benedictine nun of one of the suppressed Italian Convents.

It is not our intention to pollute our pages by quoting long extracts from this most infamous production; we shall merely touch upon a few, holding back assertions which are so vile that we should feel degraded by copying them.

"That the class of persons immured in convents," says this most venal writer, "is one useless to society, all know; but that is not enough. I have proposed, by unveiling the intimacy of their lives, to exhibit this class as even baneful to it," &c., &c.

Now every well-informed person is perfectly aware, that even in the most contemplative orders, if they do not educate, the nuns are adepts in the most delicate kinds of embroidery on satin, velvet, &c. That they make lace, and work for the poor, in addition to their own manual labor about the convent. In those less contemplative, such as the Benedictines, Augustinians, &c., &c., they devote themselves to the education of the middling and higher classes; others again have the charge of poor-schools, reformatories, hospitals; and on the sisters of charity and mercy devolve the visitation of the sick. Indeed, an idle nun would be an anomaly in the cloister, in every one of which, whether at home or abroad, industry is a paramount obligation. Truly the writer of this infamous book must have special intercourse with the father of lies, for false as are the assertions generally brought against the calumniated inmates of the cloister, she invents a fresh novelty; to wit,—

"Beneath their habit of coarse woollen serge, they wear one of the finest linen, and use handkerchiefs of the finest cambric. Also, their rosaries are mounted in silver gilt, and their vow of poverty permits them three mattresses of the softest wool, and feather pillows bordered with antique lace. The curtains, sometimes superb, are suspended from a ring in the ceiling."

We really in our consummate ignorance of conventical life, though many months the inmate of a religious house, the order of which was somewhat austere, and quite *au fait* of the life led in such establishments both in England and on the

Continent, had no idea that nuns led such comfortable, nay, luxurious lives. What a pity that Victor Emmanuel should have suppressed such flourishing and luxurious homes.

"I had been denounced before the abbess as a reader of mundane literature, and a spy having informed her, I was caught *en flagrant delit* with the book in my hand."

"What good book is this you are reading, my daughter? Let me look at it," said she.

"There being no time to conceal it, I was obliged to hand it to her, not without a lively disquietude concerning my justification of such a possession. The abbess put on her spectacles, and having read the title, restored me the closed volume, saying, 'The Memoirs of St. Helena—ah, the life of St. Constantine's mother.'"

"It was a memorial of St. Helena; and a little later I satisfied myself that the eminent superior of San Gregorio was entirely innocent of the name and fame of Napoleon the Great."

The poor lady abbess may not have been an educated woman, but we cannot believe that any person of any nation whatsoever could be ignorant of the name of Napoleon Buonaparte. The author has already told us such monstrous falsehoods that no credence can possibly be placed upon her word.

She speaks of the forms of insanity peculiar to nuns, and of the terrors of a night passed with one who was raving mad. This terrible calamity is alike horrible, whether the sufferer be in the world or the cloister; and a word *en passant*—but very recently a story went the round of the press to the effect that a nun had been forcibly carried away from a certain convent in the metropolis, and removed to the Continent, being dragged away, it was alleged, for some iniquitous purpose. It was satisfactorily proved, a little later, that the lady in question was a raving lunatic, suffering from acute mania, and that she was being conveyed to St. Julien's, a house in Bruges, under the inspection of the Belgian government. This terrible malady is as likely, of course, to fall upon a nun as upon those living in the world; and it is to be hoped that measures will be taken to secure charitable co-operation for founding a Catholic asylum in England for the cure of insanity, especially for religious, who may be suffering under this awful malady.

But to return to our Memoirs.

A few words more about this pernicious book. She gravely tells us that "convents include thieves." "A pupil had left her key in her drawer, and five piastres disappeared. A coffee service belonging to another had every silver spoon abstracted. A silver holy-water stoup, which stood at the head of my bed, was stolen from myself."

O Henrietta! Henrietta! how much, and how safely, you must count on the well-known gullibility of poor, credulous John Bull, when you can invent such stupid lies as these.

Pupils in convent schools are *never* allowed to lock drawers, closets, or boxes; if they were, what would become of the surveillance exercised in conventual establishments? where would be the neatness and regularity enjoined by the strict discipline of a conventual life? and, above all, how could the religious prevent, as effectually as they do, the introduction of bad books, or of clandestine correspondence, such as is known to be the case in our English boarding-schools, which are sometimes the hotbeds of juvenile corruption?

Henrietta Caracciolo's falsehoods are wholesale. What shall we say of the young lady pupil who owns a coffee service, from which every silver spoon was abstracted, but that falsehood is on the very face of the thing? for, in a convent school, a young lady brings with her what is necessary, nothing more—viz., a silver knife, fork, and spoon, for her *own use*.

In the cell of a nun such a thing as a silver holy-water stoup would not be allowed.

We turn with deep disgust from this tissue of stupid and absurd falsehood, deeply lamenting that, in this boasted age of enlightenment and civilization, any should be found *credulous* enough to believe in such *monstrous* inventions.

We are not at all surprised that the woman who can invent falsehoods so atrocious, hastened to break her vow of chastity, and got married.

But, after all, England *is* a land of plain speaking; and we claim at the hands of those of our country-people who may peruse these pages the same hearing which has been freely accorded to the Italian lady who penned these mendacious Memoirs.

We passed some time in one of these maligned convents; it was, too, a strictly enclosed order on the Continent; in short, one of our characters, Miss Arlington, tells *our* experience of convent life. When we say that this character *tells our own tale*, we presume nothing more will be required.

All observe the same vows, all are governed by the rules of their respective orders; and though— for they are but human—they may fall far short of the mark, still they are all bound to aim at perfection.

As an Englishwoman, we claim a hearing; and we boldly assert, that the "Memoirs of Henrietta Caracciolo" are unworthy of the credit of any *enlightened* and *well-informed* Englishman.

LIFE IN THE CLOISTER;

OR,

Faithful and True.

CHAPTER I.

AN ENGLISH HOME.

Some eight years since, before the commencement of the panic occasioned by the disastrous cotton famine, which has shaken the greatest of our commercial towns to its centre, there lived in the pretty suburb of Bowden, in the environs of Manchester, a gentleman named Craig, with his two daughters, Lilian and Marion.

This gentleman as his name will denote, was Scotch by extraction, and his family had always been members of the Episcopal Church; as to his own religious belief, he could not be said to have possessed any, save a few speculative opinions of his own; holding, indeed, the great fundamental doctrines of Christianity, but then diverging off into a species of practical atheism; the particular creed of Archibald Craig being, as he was wont facetiously to express himself, to injure no man; but, on the contrary, help his neighbor whenever it was in his power so to do.

Mr. Craig was one of the merchant princes of the great cotton district. The Laurels, as the mansion was termed in which he resided, was one of the handsomest and best kept for miles around; his horses were of the finest breed; his carriages unexceptionable; and lastly, though by no means the least, for they ought to have been mentioned first, his daughters were true Lancashire witches, or, to speak to the point, two of the loveliest young women one might ever chance to meet with.

A word, though, *en passant.*

Surely this term of Lancashire witches, taken in the sense in which it is generally used, is not a fair one; for the palm of beauty, if applied collectively, can by no rule of justice be given, or said to be, the distinctive mark of the ladies of Lancashire above the female sex in the other counties of England; on an average, we fancy, from what we have seen of its maids and matrons during a residence of some years amongst them, that there are about the same number of pretty faces to be met with there, neither more nor less, as in any other county in the British isles.

It is not often that we meet with a face which can be termed *correctly* beautiful, yet such was that of Lilian, the eldest of Mr. Craig's daughters.

Marion, the younger sister, also had uncommon pretensions to physical beauty, but her features wanted the regularity which her sister's possessed.

Shall we describe these two young women whose fortunes form the subject of this narrative? We think not—such descriptions are hackneyed·; so the reader will please merely to imagine the countenances of these two sisters very unlike as to features, and yet like as to expression; the elder, Lilian, with her dazzlingly-fair complexion, dark eyes and hair, somewhat stately as to figure and outward bearing; and her sister, sweet Marion Craig, with sunny locks and violet eyes, her figure more *petite* than that of her sister, full of all the guileless *abandon* of a young and innocent woman, her countenance the very soul of animation and good temper. Such were these young ladies of Bowden in the year 1856. But we have to speak of the mental endowments of these girls more than of their natural graces. They were the admiration of all Manchester; the belles of the last London season, their hands were sought in marriage by wealthy men; nay, it was rumored that the stately Lilian might have had a coronet had she chosen to accept it; but the wilful maiden chose to remain still plain Lilian Craig, to her father's intense displeasure.

Beautiful, amiable, and good, what *could* Mr. Craig desire more? Alas, alas! there is a skeleton in every house; these poor young ladies formed the source of domestic unhappiness to the rich millocrat.

Let us peep in at him as he sits in the library in that stately home at Bowden; he is all alone; the two wilful, wayward girls, on whom all his hopes have rested, have both left him in tears.

"Was ever man so deceived? was ever father so troubled? This comes of having a couple of daughters, forsooth—both of them to fly in my face in this way."

Mr. Craig got up and paced up and down the room; his books had no charms that night, and he was still bewailing his hard lot in having two such perverse daughters, when the sound of carriage wheels struck upon his ear, and a very old friend, a wealthy mill-owner like himself, by name John Gilmour, was shown into the room.

"Glad to see you; 'pon my honor never was better pleased to see you in my life," said Mr. Craig, seizing his friend by the hand, and warmly shaking it. "I want your advice; those girls of mine are the greatest trouble to me, now that I had thought all trouble was over with them. I have ordered them both out of the room; their conduct is undutiful to the last degree."

"Lilian and Marion a trouble to you!" exclaimed his friend; "why, surely you jest, Craig. I have always thought them models of filial duty."

"Filial duty!—a fig for such duty as my precious daughters show to me," answered the enraged father. "Tell me, Gilmour, if it is not enough to drive any man in his senses mad. First, you are aware Miss Lilian chose to refuse the offer of Lord

Strathmore, as if it were no honor for the daughter of a poor commoner to be raised out of her own rank in life; and at last it turns out, when I insist upon knowing *why* she has chosen so pertinaciously to refuse another eligible offer, that she has chosen, without consulting me at all about the matter, to want to marry that poor artist, Herbert Leslie, forsooth, who has not a cent to bless himself with. There now," he added, "I just ask you if it is not enough to drive a man mad, at the very moment when he thinks his troubles as a father are about to cease by his child's settlement in life, to find that they are all about to begin?"

"My dear fellow," said Mr. Gilmour, leaning his head on his hand, and looking very grave, "a man's troubles may only be said to begin when his children are fairly grown up, and the question of a settlement for life comes on the *tapis*. Listen to an old family man, Craig, with five sons and seven daughters, all of whom Providence has willed should '*grow up like olive plants around his table,*' as the Psalmist hath it; listen to me, Craig," he added, placing his folded hands on the table, and assuming a still more serious expression of countenance, "and believe me when I tell you, it is now, when I look around on all these young men and women, that I feel the full weight of the fearful, nay, the *awful* nature of the responsibility I incurred when I became a husband and a father. But, however, you're a rich man, Craig; I should advise you to submit; let her have Herbert; my young people are going a *widely* different road to that I had marked out; but they must make a kirk or a mill of it, Craig. I must yield—can't stand out; too much trouble to stand out, my good fellow."

"I pity you, Gilmour; from my very soul I pity you," said Craig, suddenly pausing in his walk up and down the apartment, a practice Mr. Craig always indulged in when he was at all disturbed. "I shan't follow *your* example, Gilmour. These good-for-nothing girls break my rest, and I'll break their *hearts*, but what I'll break their present resolutions."

"So much for Lilian, my good fellow," responded Gilmour, shrugging his shoulders; "but what about my friend Marion; she is my god-daughter? I have a right, you know, to give advice in that quarter, so out with it, gossip;—how has Marion offended you?"

"She is worse than her sister, Gilmour; infinitely worse," exclaimed Craig, striking his clenched fist violently on the table as he spoke. "She is for ever whining, and fretting, and pestering me out of my life to let her take herself off into a convent, of all places in the world. I don't admire such fancies, and never did. She goes into no convent, I can tell her."

"A convent," replied Gilmour, musingly; "why, when was she seized with that fancy?"

"Oh, the blessed effects of a convent education, to be sure. I allowed my poor wife to send both the girls to some one of these Notre Dame convents at Canley Heath, close to London. You know the place—it ranks rather high amongst the houses of their institute; and this is the precious fruit of my folly. I declare I'm driven mad with their whims and fancies. I don't admire, I never did, the practice of giving stepmothers to grown-up daughters; but I really begin to think that a little wholesome subordination of that kind would have done both of them good. What shall I do, Gilmour?" added the poor, perplexed old gentleman, leaning his head on his hand, and looking anxiously at his friend.

"Let them go their own gait, man; that is my advice," replied Gilmour. "Herbert Leslie is poor at present, it is true, but he may rise in his profession, and he is an excellent young man after all; and as to my pretty godchild, Marion, why, let her be happy in her own way, and go to Canley, if she wishes to do so."

"Friend Gilmour," replied Mr. Craig, with more vehemence than he had hitherto spoken, "it is the old story, the way with almost the whole world—I have asked your advice, and it does not please me, so I mean to follow my own."

"Bless me, man, I think you have lost your senses," exclaimed Gilmour, somewhat irritated at the rudeness of his old friend; "but shake hands, Craig," he said, extending his hand as he spoke; "and don't follow my advice unless it seems good to you; I only say what I should do had I wilful lasses."

"Well, don't go away, Gilmour," said Craig, "let's talk about business matters. It will do me good to banish the girls from my mind for a little while; and I'll find some way to punish them both later. Ah, by the way, I have it!" he said, pausing for a moment, as if a happy idea had occurred to him. "They are both anxious"—

"I thought you had decided on dismissing these refractory girls from your mind for the present," interrupted Gilmour, laughing. "I was just going to ask if there was any change in the cotton market."

"All in good time; but I was about to say," replied the angry father, "if you'll let me speak without interrupting me, that Lilian has been plaguing me to take her to London, and so has Marion. I told them I would do so; but I see through their plan. Leslie has returned to his family, who are residing at Brixton, I believe. I may say, *en passant*, they are all as poor as church mice; then, of course, Miss Marion would only be about an hour's walk from the Heath. Well, my young ladies, instead of going to London, then, I'll punish you both by starting you off to Lytham. That sober, quiet little watering-place shall sober you both into your senses and obedience to your father's will, or I'll know the reason why before I have done with you.—Now to the state of the cotton market," he hurriedly added, as if afraid that his friend should again espouse the cause of the rebellious damsels.

Mr. Craig was naturally as quick tempered as his easy-going friend was the reverse. Mr. Craig gloried when there was a dispute betwixt himself and Mr. Gilmour, which happened not unfrequently to be the case, in being able to show that he had the power as well as the will to punish those who had offended him.

We doubt if there be anything more annoying to hasty persons than an unwise recapitulation of real or fancied grievances to those who, perhaps by nature rather than any superior virtue, scarce know what it is to feel an impulse of anger. Oscott had been the *alma mater* of each of these two men; they had grown up from boyhood together, had become bosom friends, located themselves in the same county, engaged in the same branch of commerce, and had continued good friends; though we may not deny that occasionally the peaceful nature of their intercourse was marred by some little outbreak of temper on the part of the irascible Mr. Craig, who was wont often to say—

"If I speak rudely to Gilmour, it is his own fault; he never *will* see wrong where wrong exists; if the man would but agree with me, I should not be half so violent as I am."

This was quite true. It is extremely likely, that if Mr. Gilmour had blamed these unreasonable young ladies, who wanted to be happy in a fashion that was displeasing to papa, Mr. Craig would have cooled down, instead of taking matters with so high a hand; as it was it only made things worse.

Thus, after a few minutes chat with his friend, he suddenly rose from the table, and rung the bell violently, saying,—

"Nothing like striking the iron while it's hot; eh, friend Gilmour? The punishment of my daughters shall begin to-night."

A servant out of livery answered his summons.

"Go to Mrs. Whiteside, immediately, John, and tell her I wish her to let the young ladies know that they are to leave home for Lytham by the nine o'clock train to-morrow morning, and to see that they have everything in readiness. Now, my dear girls, you will shed a few tears to-night," said the old gentleman, chuckling with pleasure. "Lytham instead of London is the proper place for you. Go on, Gilmour. I think you were saying that your usual complement of hands at the mill could scarce get through their work."

"Yes, you severe old paterfamilias, I was saying so," said Gilmour, with a laugh; "but for the life of you, you could not hear me quietly out."

CHAPTER II.

THE TWO SISTERS, AND HOW THEY BORE THEIR PUNISHMENT.

THERE was one room at the Laurels, in the fitting up of which Mr. Craig had spared no expense. This was the boudoir of his late wife, and it was now specially devoted to the use of Lilian and her sister. The hangings and curtains were of pale blue satin, looped and fringed with silver; the fauteuils and cushions were all covered with the same material; two French windows gave egress to a beautiful conservatory, filled with the rarest exotics; tables of ivory, inlaid with silver, and bearing—but by no means inconveniently crowded together to the exclusion of good taste—many a curious gem of art, purchased at various times, for the gratification of the wife whom he had idolised.

Lilian and her sister were intellectual. This their special apartment betrayed their taste for the fine arts, in the elegant little piano, the harp, whose chords Lilian loved to awaken, and the correct authors, whose works, gorgeously bound, lay scattered around the room.

Strange that these two sisters should be unhappy.

All that wealth could give was theirs; they were devotedly attached to each other, and were dearly loved by an affectionate father; but other loves had sprung up, and discord had entered into their home; the shadow which had lately cast itself over their path now lengthened before them. For the first time in their lives, these girls were unhappy.

"Papa has seemed to be so partial to Herbert," said Lilian, "that I never thought he would be so angry when I asked for his consent to our union."

At this moment, Mrs. Whiteside entered the room, and delivered Mr. Craig's message.

"Lytham!" exclaimed both young ladies in the same breath; "you must be making a mistake, Mrs. Whiteside; papa promised to take us to London the end of the week."

"I assure you I am making no mistake, Miss Craig," replied the housekeeper. "John says that your papa distinctly said you were to leave home for Lytham by the nine o'clock train to-morrow morning. I am now going to tell Benson to get your things in readiness, Miss; and there is such a short time to make preparations in. It is a great pity Mr. Craig did not tell us earlier in the day."

The housekeeper withdrew, and the young ladies exchanged glances expressive of both surprise and dissatisfaction.

Lilian, the most impetuous, was the first to speak.

"I shall go to my father, and tell him that it is impossible that we can leave at the time he has fixed. What *can* he be thinking of, to hurry us off to a humdrum watering-place, when he had promised we should go to London. No chance of seeing Herbert now," she added. "I will go to my father at once."

"You won't alter his resolution one bit, Lilian," said Marion, the bright tear-drops glistening in her eye. "I am persuaded he has changed his plans for the express purpose of distressing us. Nay, how can you be so silly, Lilian," she added; "you know what papa is when he is thoroughly out of temper. I am quite as disappointed as ever you can be; for I had promised myself a few happy days at Canley; but I am far too proud to let papa think he distresses me so much; for the fact is, Lilian, he punishes us as if we were children, by such freaks as these—forgetting we are women."

"O Marion, Marion, what *would* Sister Pauline say did she hear you talk like this? What a spirit of insubordination! You've not learned your first lesson in humility yet, that is quite certain."

Marion prevailed, as was always the case when the sisters did happen to differ,—a circumstance, by the way, which did not often occur; indeed, it was a marvel how these two should ever have resolved on separation, so devotedly attached were they to each other; only, as we have before said, other loves had sprung up in their hearts.

On the following morning, the sisters appeared as usual at the breakfast-table, resolved to play out their part to the last, if possible. Lilian, however, succeeded but very imperfectly. Mr. Craig was full of a mischievous pleasure at the idea of the mortification and disappointment he had occasioned his daughters, and his first words were—

"All ready, I hope, girls; we start in less than an hour," he added, looking at his watch. "I flatter myself I have given you both a pleasant surprise; satisfied that you will enjoy yourselves much more at the sea-side than in London; and confident that Marion especially will feel grateful for the chance I have afforded her for three months' quiet seclusion, so befitting for a preparation to the holy life she fancies herself called upon to enter— but how now, Lilian, what is the matter with you?" he exclaimed, seeing her face flush crimson with her ill-concealed effort to suppress her temper, and that then she burst into tears, unable to bear his badinage any longer.

"O papa!" she said, "you know well how I hate the country; I am no hypocrite. *Why* are you taking us to Lytham, when you had promised us a month in London?"

"Mistress Lilian," said the old gentleman, heated with temper, yet speaking with the greatest coolness, and still indulging in the same satirical vein, "Mistress Lilian, I judge three months spent in the quiet retirement of Lytham the very fittest thing for both of you. I shall spend every Sunday with you, and"—

"Three months!" exclaimed both Lilian and Marion in the same breath. The latter, heaving a deep sigh, said no more; but Lilian, who inherited her father's quick, impulsive temper, added—

"Three months, father! what *are* you thinking of? You are jesting with us; but I am like yourself, and do not like to be laughed at, I candidly tell you. I shall die of *ennui*, if you condemn me to such odious retirement for the term you have mentioned."

"Let it bring you both to your senses, then," said her father, making the table ring with the violence with which he struck his clenched fist upon it. "Three whole months shall pass before you shall either of you return to Bowden; and as for London, why, you'll neither of you go there for one year at least."

Lilian pushed her cup and plate aside. She was too indignant to speak; but she chafed inwardly at the idea of her own helplessness. As to Marion, brave Marion, proud Marion, she kept a guard upon herself, mindful of the truth of that quaint old adage which says, "What can't be cured must be endured."

A little later, and Mr. Craig, with a daughter on each arm, alighted from his carriage at the railway station; and, to tell the truth, those generally affectionate daughters had felt desperately disinclined to take the proffered arm.

Seats were taken in a first-class carriage, and they were walking down the platform, when the two Miss Elliots—women who were no favorites with the young ladies—espied them.

"Is it possible, Mr. Craig, that you are leaving Bowden for Lytham?" exclaimed the elder of the two. "Why, I did not think we should lose you so soon; we understood you were going to spend part of the season in London."

"So I had intended, madam," replied the old gentleman; "but circumstances, you see, make us often change our plans. There are some little points at variance between myself and my daughters; and when young people are out of temper I always fancy their bodily health is affected; so with a view to mend both the one and the other, I intend my daughters to ruralise for three months at Lytham."

"Three months!" ejaculated Miss Elliot; "why, my dear Lilian, you will not like it—you who detest the country so much. Mr. Craig, you are severe. I am afraid, with your amiable daughters, Lytham is the very *ne plus ultra* of all that is quiet."

"The very place, madam, for thought and reflection," replied the mischievous old gentleman; "but hark! there is the bell; we must wish you good-bye," he added, as he held open the carriage-door, in order that his daughters might take possession of their seats. Even Marion's eyes flashed with indignation, whilst Lilian was boiling over. She flung herself into a seat, exclaiming—

"O papa, you are very cruel.! Surely it was enough to drag us from Bowden, without making all Bowden merry with the news that we were being punished like a couple of children."

"I am glad you feel it, Lilian; it is all for your good; but not another word," he said, enjoining silence with his finger on his lips. "Do not expose yourself before strangers." Never did ride in a railway carriage seem more dreary to the two sisters than was this; added to which, their pride had been wounded in the tenderest point by the knowledge that their father was dealing with them as if the days of their early girlhood were to be lived over again.

At last the sight of the shipping in the old dock made known to them that they were nearing Lytham, a pretty place, which they had never visited, but which had been described to them by a dissipated, pleasure-loving family of their acquaintance, as remarkably quiet and *ennuyante*.

They were now to judge for themselves. A few moments more, and the train steamed into the neat and pretty station; and, on alighting, Mr. Craig, unusually attentive and polite to his daughters, because particularly irritated against them, again tendered his arm, and turned his steps in the direction of the beach, his daughters lost in wonder at the step he was about to take; for on former occasions, whenever the merchant prince had patronised watering-places, he had always engaged a large and commodious house, bringing with him his carriage, and five or six servants.

Not so on the present occasion. Mr. Craig's temper was still at fever heat; and, when this was the case, he always took especial care to make the offender suffer. How much more readily, then, could he effect his purpose, when the offenders were, as in the present case, his own children.

It was certainly laughable enough in its way, this idea of punishing two young women as if they were naughty children; but it was no laughing matter for his victims; for, though there was seemingly nothing at issue beyond a few months' dwelling in a pretty watering-place, you see it involved a tedious separation from those in whose society they wished to mix, and to Lilian, especially, an absolute want of the pleasure and amusements she had pictured to herself as about to enjoy.

Turning the corner of the Station Road, Mr. Craig looked right and left, whilst Marion quietly admired the very beautiful beach, with the blue waters beyond, and a few sailing vessels in the distance, plying between Liverpool and Preston. Turning to the right, he bent his steps towards a row of small but extremely pretty cottages, or rather villas, made, like all the other buildings, of red brick, with pretty casement windows, the walls covered over with creeping plants. The roofs of these villas were pointed, and before the houses stretched very neat gardens, tastefully laid out,

each with a miniature lawn. In the bay window
of one of these cottages hung a bill, containing the
announcement that there were "Apartments to
Let;" and, to the surprise and ineffable disgust of
Lilian, her father opened the garden-gate in order
to make his inquiries. Was this, then, the place
in which he meant to leave them? vastly pretty,
exquisitely clean, but quite unfit for the daughters
of the rich Mr. Craig. Was no carriage to be sent
down, not even the pony phaeton? she asked, as,
all arrangements concluded, and a parlor and two
sleeping-rooms engaged, Mr. Craig informed them
that he should lunch with them, and then return
to Manchester.

"The carriage or phaeton!" he said, as if
astonished at the question. "Certainly not. If he
were with them, the case would be different; but
young ladies—who wished, the one to marry a
poor man, who could scarcely pay the hire of a cab,
and the other, who wanted to be a nun—had no
need of carriages to drive in; they could walk on
foot."

A deep sigh was the only reply of Marion. As
to Lilian, she was too indignant to suffer herself to
speak; and, after a half-hour's walk on the beach,
they returned home to lunch, during which the
father and daughters scarcely exchanged a dozen
words together.

"Mrs. Wilson," he said, addressing the landlady,
when about to take his departure, "you will have
the goodness to let my daughters have whatever

they require, and get the bill ready for me to settle when I come here on Saturday."

There was no choice but to accompany Mr. Craig to the Station; and, for once in their lives, they parted from their father with feelings of suppressed indignation.

Lilian returned to the cottage in company with her sister, declaring that she could not breathe in that small parlor, the ceiling of which was so low. She termed the place "a little Holland," with nothing to be seen, save a dingy old mill, turning its sails round whenever she went to the window; grew angry with Marion, and outrageous with Benson, because they could not view things with the same jaundiced eye; called her father a *brute*, who did all he could think of to make her miserable; and, after pacing the room in a fit of uncontrollable anger, threw herself on the couch, and wept herself to sleep.

Then Marion, turning to Benson,—a staid, demure woman of some forty years of age, who had been her deceased mother's maid—begged her to put on her cloak and bonnet, and come with her to explore the place, adding, "Lilian will not miss us for a good two hours, Benson; she has fallen into a deep sleep. My heart is very heavy; I shall feel better if I can but get out."

Benson—who really loved both sisters, but Marion in particular—was soon ready; and out they went, turning their steps towards the west beach. It was a lovely afternoon towards the end of June, not too warm to prevent their walk from being a pleasant one. The place looked exceedingly pretty, with its *cottages ornees* and villas, trimly-kept gardens and ornamental palisades in front; whilst beyond lay the beach, perhaps one of the finest in England, the turf with which it was covered bright as an emerald in its freshness; and a little further the promenade, the sands beneath now washed over by the tide, which was rapidly coming in.

There was an air of quietude and peace over the place, which, though she was brought to it so reluctantly, fascinated Marion even against her will. Under other circumstances, this would have been the very spot she would have liked; for, inasmuch as Lilian loved the crowded streets and busy thoroughfares of a thronged city, so did Marion love the quiet scenes of the country. She seated herself on a bench, and sat for some time, enjoying the scene, admiring the light sailing vessels, skimming, as it were, the surface of the waters; whilst ever and anon a sea-gull dipped its white wings in the crested waves, and then soared high above them; and as she sat musing over yesterday's quarrel with her father, and her sudden removal to this place, she began to reproach herself severely for the irritation she had felt, acknowledging to herself the truth that, quiet as were her habits and pursuits, Lytham would have been a pleasant place to her, but for the circumstances under which she had become a resident there.

She, however, dreaded what she knew both herself and Benson would have to encounter from the temper of Lilian, and expected to find her still asleep, or, if not, chafing, fretting, and pacing up and down the room, as she had done before she left her.

She was then somewhat surprised to see Lilian, beautiful Lilian, sitting at the table writing—writing, with a smile on her lip, and seemingly in the best of spirits.

"Well, my dear, have you seen anything to amuse yourself in this deserted little Holland?" she said, as her sister entered the room.

"O Lilian, Lilian, how fond you are of crowded streets! Look now; can you see no superior beauty in the fair prospect before you, with the setting sun tipping with its golden light the surface of the deep. How can you prefer the noisy, dusty streets to the calm quiet of this place!—you, with all your intellect;—it *does* surprise me, Lilian."

"Be surprised, my love," replied her sister; "it is quite right and proper, and not at all astonishing, that *you*, whose every wish is to become a nun, should admire the country; but give to me, as I have always told you, the bustle and tumult, and the active life, of a crowded city, with all its pleasures and amusements, Marion,—give me its concert-rooms and theatres in the week, and on the Sunday its spacious churches and their beautiful ceremonials. O Marion, I would like to pass all my life in Paris or in London."

The younger sister looked wonderingly at her, and sighed, saying—

"Mercy on me, Lilian, what a medley of things you have put together. Oh, do reflect; and ask yourself, if, with your taste for all that is gay and expensive, you will be a happy wife should you wed Herbert Leslie?"

"Yes, I should," was the reply. "Look here," and she held up the sheet of paper on which she had been writing; "this note goes to Brixton by the evening post."

"Dear Lilian," said Marion, passing her arm around her sister's waist, "remember papa has forbidden correspondence with Herbert; be prudent; wait, Lilian; for heaven's sake, wait. Our very residence here, in this to you distasteful place, should warn you of what he is capable should you grievously offend him. Wait and watch, Lilian; do *you* wait till Herbert has time to secure his own prospects in life; and I will wait, aye, wait if needs be for years, and yet patiently work out my wish at last."

"This letter goes to-night, Marion," said the self-willed girl. "Look you now, my father should not visit my failings with such severity. I read his character in my own hasty temperament, my own obstinacy, if you please to give it so harsh a name; but to relieve you of your fears, I will just own to you that this letter is *not* written to Herbert, as my father has chosen to forbid my correspondence; oh no, it is only to his favorite sister, Kate; that will answer my purpose just as well. I have simply told her that papa has quarrelled with both of us, and also the reason why we are punished by being sent here, forsooth."

"Lilian, dearest, I feel very unhappy. Mark my words, evil will come of that letter."

"I am quite ready to meet the evil, darling. Now let me finish it," she said; "and tell Benson to be ready to go with me to the post, for I will not even trust *her* with it, lest she should be tormented with any scruple about my father, and dare send it on to him instead; he may have put our very maid as a spy on our actions, Marion. How inconceivably humbled I felt at his leaving us without money, and even telling the mistress of this house to get what we required, and make out her bill to him."

To expostulate was useless. Marion went up to her little bedroom, how little to that at Bowden, with its elegant appointments; her sister's conversation had again lighted up the smouldering embers which yet smothered in her own breast; *she* even looked out disdainfully at the pretty landscape; regarded her father in the light of a tyrant; remembered that she had seen handsome and spacious houses on the west beach, whilst he had located them in this small cottage; that he had never left them before without an abundant supply of money, never deprived them of the use of an equipage. And though Marion knew that all these things could be well dispensed with, and that *she* especially should not desire them, if she wished to imbibe the true spirit of the state she aimed at; yet she regarded the loss of them as a proof of despotic tyranny on the part of her father, saying to herself—

"He was young once upon a time. I wonder how he would have borne it had his father forbade his marriage with my mother; or how he would have liked it, had he wished to devote himself to the Church, and had his desires thwarted? Parental tyranny, domestic misrule," added the rebellious daughter; "no music here, no books, I declare; only two or three I caught up in the hurry of our departure. *How shall* we wile away our time!"

My lady readers don't be too severe on these rebellious young damsels. Their characters are not very estimable in the days of their prosperity; but they will be refined in the crucible of adversity, and come through the fiery ordeal like purified gold.

Day after day wore on very monotonously, till the Saturday on which, agreeably to his promise, Mr. Craig arrived. Lilian had not yet had an answer to her letter, consequently she was still in the old mood, and felt somewhat like a restive young horse, unwilling and yet obliged to submit to the superior power which governs him. Marion, too, was out of spirits. She had written a letter to the sisters at Canley; it had not been answered. It was very unkind of them to neglect her so, whispered Marion's proud spirit. You see she was beginning to lose *her* temper as well as Lilian; so that when their despotic lord arrived, the two ladies made but little show of concealing what they felt. Mr. Craig arrived at the station, with many other Manchester gentlemen, by the four o'clock train. Their wives and daughters were waiting for them on the platform; and before he alighted from the carriage, he regarded with a feeling of fatherly pride his two beautiful daughters. He noticed, however, from the expression of their countenances, that the novel punishment with which he had visited them had taken effect; for the stately Lilian looked wonderfully as if she repressed her tears only by a marvellous effort, as well as his usually gay, bright-eyed Marion.

"All right," he muttered to himself; "the way to serve girls who, with wealth and good looks, are intent on such a future as they carve out for themselves."

The evening passed away very drearily. Mr. Craig had dropped the tone of badinage he had assumed when he took them from Manchester, but did not fail to annoy them; and he hoped his communication would have that effect, by informing them that the Misses Elliot would visit Lytham the following week, adding—

"Lytham is the best place in England for delicate people. I have advised them to come; and they have promised me that they will call and see you as soon as they arrive."

"I do not want to see that spiteful, censorious

Miss Elliott," thundered out Lilian. "You know how much I dislike her, papa. I am very sorry she is coming here at all; and to see us in this place too—so small, so confined, after our spacious rooms at Bowden; it is a wonder that Marion and myself are not both ill."

Mr. Craig vouchsafed no reply, except that he had asked the Misses Elliott as a personal favor to visit his daughters, and should insist that they were properly received. The following day was Sunday. They attended mass in the pretty little chapel of the place, were duly edified by the piety of the congregation, and returning home at a still early hour in the morning, found the day insupportably long upon their hands.

In the afternoon, however, Mr. Craig, himself a great walker, suggested a ramble to the Star Hills, as they are called; and then dragged the young ladies far on the way to Blackpool, till, thoroughly worn out, Lilian declared she should drop down from fatigue, unless she returned home at once.

The long, in fact too long, walk was however not unprofitable; it made them both so drowsy that the weary day was shortened by each of them falling asleep during more than two hours of the evening. Mr. Craig was very foolish, to say the least, or he would have known, as a good priest once quaintly expressed it, "that idleness was the Evil One's work-shop." He was merciless in the species of tyranny he unwisely indulged in; and when Lilian, always the spokeswoman, requested that her musical instruments should be sent down, with a parcel of her favorite authors, he replied in the negative, saying—

"I wish to accustom you both to do without all and each one of the comforts by which you have been surrounded. You will have nothing here beyond absolute necessaries. Herbert can furnish you with nothing more. I wish to see how you can bear the change."

"And for how long?" she said. "Never for three months! Remember, that were I Herbert's wife to-morrow, were Marion a nun this day, our hands and minds would not be thus unoccupied."

"In three months from the day I brought you here you will return to Bowden; and if you really find the time pass so very slowly, hire a piano; that, and that alone, is the only indulgence I shall afford to either of you," said Mr. Craig, coldly touching the foreheads of his daughters with his lips, as he bade them good-bye.

CHAPTER III.

TREATS OF UNWELCOME VISITORS, AND A WARM RECEPTION.

SURE enough, early in the week came to Lytham the two stiff, demure ladies, whose rigid views had always been the terror of the Misses Craig. Severe in their notions of right to a positive fault, making no allowance for the failings of others, unforgiving when offended, censorious and rigidly exact in their own conduct, they won but little love in the little coterie in which they moved.

As to religion, it was presented in their own persons, in a very sour and forbidding aspect, depriving it of all that renders it sweet and pleasant, investing it with the dark coloring lent by their own morose bigotry.

With these ladies it was a sin to indulge in innocent recreation, to enter a place of amusement, to read a work of imagination. It was simply wonderful how such persons could have ever submitted themselves to the benign influences of the Catholic faith; and they had certainly brought into the Church the puritanical tendencies imbibed in their early years from a certain Mrs. Donald, their maternal grand-mother, and the wife of a Scottish

Presbyterian, with whom their youth had been spent.

Such were the ladies whose society was in a manner forced upon Lilian and her sister. They had taken apartments in one of the largest houses on the beach, and drove up in their own carriage to the gate of the unassuming but pretty cottage in which the sisters lodged.

"Here are those odious Miss Elliots," exclaimed Lilian, starting from the couch. "I shall leave you to receive them, Marion," she said, rushing from the room. "I feel as if I could not be civil to those women."

But Lilian did not effect her escape so cleverly as she thought, for the voluminous skirt of her muslin dress was still visible as her light form turned the corner of the little staircase facing the hall-door; and the impropriety of a young lady rushing with such vulgar haste from the room, because she beheld visitors coming, was duly descanted on by the elder of the two ladies.

"Why, Marion," said Miss Elliot, "we were so surprised that papa should have brought you here. He was so pleased to hear that we were coming, and begged us to see you very often, so that we consider it a positive duty to look after you both; we shall see you *every* day without fail, calling each morning to give you a drive in our carriage, and then shall either spend the afternoon and evening with you, or expect you to be with us."

Marion bowed assent, and tried—deceitful Marion

—tried to look pleased, when she felt as if she should burst into tears.

At last Lilian entered the room, and the two repellant natures—the one cold and stately, the other stiff and forbidding—came in contact with each other.

"I thank you," she replied, as Miss Elliot reiterated her offers of acting as a chaperone; "but I doubt if you will find my company agreeable; you know how I dislike the country; I prefer music and a few books to driving about these deserted lanes and roads."

"Strange, such a decidedly unpoetical turn of mind, my dear Lilian. However, you have a very pretty place here," she said, glancing with affected admiration round the small parlor, and mentally contrasting it with Lilian's spacious boudoir at Bowden. "Papa is always so kindly solicitous, my dear, about every thing connected with you, nothing is too good; Martha has often made that observation; have you not, Martha?" she added, glancing towards her sister.

"Oh, no doubt, no doubt," replied Lilian, with somewhat of asperity, "papa always acts for the best, however things may turn out."

Then, starting from her seat, with such sudden impetuosity that the staid and quiet Martha's nerves were terribly shaken, she rushed to the bell-rope, rang it with a haste only warrantable if one of the ladies had fallen into a fainting fit, and bade Benson put wine and cake on the table, to the immense surprise of the visitors, and the uncontrollable mirth of Marion.

"My dear Lilian, how you do surprise me! Bless me, why such hurry?" exclaimed Miss Elliot. "One would have thought your very life depended on the haste with which you could ring that bell. Do you not know, my love, that such impetuosity is neither in accordance with the rules of good breeding, nor with religion itself?"

"Very likely not, Miss Elliot," said Lilian, her white hand shaking as she lifted the decanter, and her big eyes sparkled with ill-concealed anger; "very likely not; but you see I care very little about what *you* term the rules of good breeding; and, what is more, I am not going even to try to become what you call a model young lady. Your model young ladies are full of affectation."

"Ah, my dear Lilian, I much fear you never will, indeed," answered the lady; "but come now, put on your hats, and take a drive with us. We are going towards Blackpool; the drive is a pretty one, I assure you."

"None of the drives are pretty," answered Lilian. "I thank you very much, Miss Elliot; but I do *so* hate the country, that I prefer trying over with Marion a new piece of music, arranged as a duet, which we have received by the morning post."

"Very well, Lilian, then I hold you excused for once in a way; but shall expect you to join us to-morrow morning; for the fresh air will do you good, if the scenery presents no charm to your eyes; added to which, I pledged my word to your father that I would not leave you young people too much alone."

As Miss Elliot spoke thus, she moved towards the door; and, ringing the bell, heartily glad to be rid of the company of the two ladies, Lilian accompanied them to the hall door. Then, returning, she went to the window, and gazed after them, as their tall, gaunt forms ascended the carriage-steps, and exclaimed—

"It is such censorious, spiteful women as you who bring odium on the single portion of our sex. I never can forgive papa for setting you both as spies on our actions, nor for the cruel humiliations he has put upon us, as if, indeed, we were children, and not able to take care of ourselves."

Matilda Elliot threw herself back in her luxurious seat, saying—

"Is it not very odd, Martha, that a man so wealthy as Craig is supposed to be should have put these girls alone, with only a maid-servant, in a cottage like that, with rooms not half the size of their own apartments at Bowden."

"It is," replied her sister. "What is the mystery, there is a skeleton in the house, depend on it, Tilda; friend Craig has only admitted us to half his confidence."

"Very strange," replied Matilda. "Is it possible things are getting shaky with him. He has been living in a most extravagant style. What if he should be near bankruptcy. The first thing he would do would be to get his proud, stuck-up Lilian, and his pretty fool Marion, right out of the way."

"I do not think your ideas at all improbable," rejoined her sister. "Miss Lilian is so impulsive that I expected she would own the truth when I spoke of her father's care for their comfort. Not a bit of it, however; I only mortified her pride. Did you notice the haste with which she rang the bell for the wine? It was nothing in the world, my dear sister, but an idle excuse to cover her suppressed passion. Mark my words, Martha,— the pride of that girl will be punished sooner or later, depend on it. Just fancy that stuck-up doll in an atmosphere of poverty; and there's nothing more likely. My dear, the change will be a terrible one, whenever it takes place. I do not like the girls; I never did, especially the eldest. However, there are two motives why we must not leave them to themselves: the first, that I promised their father to visit them every day; and the second, because, with a very natural curiosity, I am anxious to know the cause of these two girls being sent here, instead of to London. There's a mystery somewhere, I am certain."

As Miss Elliot spoke thus, the carriage stopped at their own door, and stopped also the conversation of these two amiable ladies.

We will leave them for a while, and introduce new and very different characters to the reader.

CHAPTER IV.

**THE CONVENT OF NOTRE DAME—THE ARTIST'S HOME—
AND THE FAST-GOING YOUNG LADY.**

It is a lovely evening in June. A few summer showers, in the early part of the day, have cooled the air, and drawn out the delicious perfume of the sweet-scented rose, the clove pink, and heliotrope; and glowing beds of azaleas and geraniums bend beneath the weight of the pearly drops yet hanging on their lovely flowers; and no sound breaks upon the ear save the lowing of a few cows, or the bleating of the sheep feeding on some pasture land in the distance.

We are in the grounds of the Convent of Notre Dame, on Canley Heath; and though it be only a very short distance, nay, within an easy ride of the noisy metropolis, and situated in a fashionable and wealthy suburb, yet the silence is profound.

The mansion, erst the residence of a gentleman of fortune, now converted into a convent, is spacious, you see; and those who enter, even if not already acquainted with the fact, would quickly surmise that they were in some establishment consecrated to religious uses, so profound is the stillness which reigns around, so exquisite the neatness and cleanliness of the place.

Let us wander down this long passage; pass we through the doors of stained glass which, standing so invitingly open, conduct us to the grounds, the lawn, with its fresh greensward so carefully kept, stretching right away till a huge clump of trees screens from our sight the large extent of ground beyond, as also the group of ladies with whom we are going to make acquaintance.

The postman has just left a little delicate-tinted note, with a pink seal bearing the words *Au revoir* upon its surface, and the nun whose duty it is to act as portress approaches the Sister Superior and hands her the letter.

Now the good Mother Angelique receives many a delicate and perfumed note from the fashionable and wealthy dames who place their daughters beneath the care of herself and her community, but there is evidently some anomaly here between the writer and the appearance of the dainty epistle. A smile crosses her quiet placid face as she recognizes the handwriting and the seal, and detects the perfume yet hovering on the tinted paper so recently laid within a fashionable ladies desk.

"Poor child! poor child!" she says, addressing a few of the senior nuns, who are privileged in being the nearest to her person. "See, this dainty epistle is from our old pupil, pretty Marion Craig, who begged us to join in a Novena in order that she might have the grace of a Vocation. This perfumed rosy paper savors rather strongly of the world; let us see what she has to say."

The Sister Superior opened the letter, read it to herself first, and then communicated its contents to the nuns. It ran as follows:

"DEAREST REV. MOTHER,—A great disappointment has befallen me, nay, a great trial to both myself and dear Lilian. You know that in my last I told you with much joy that I was convinced God called me to serve Him in holy religion, and that papa had promised to bring us both to London; also, that I intended to make him acquainted with the state of my feelings.

"I believe, too, you are aware that Lilian has formed an attachment with the brother of one of your old *eleves*, dear Kate Leslie. Now my father has been begging her to accept the hand of a certain nobleman, who has been paying his addresses to her; and his anger was extreme when she declared that she wished to marry Herbert; and will you, can you believe it, dearest mother? he has been no less violent with myself.

"The end of it all is, he has sent us both off to Lytham, a *very* pretty little watering-place, telling us we shall live there at least three months, till we are both cured of our folly. He has taken small rooms for us in a neat but excessively small cottage, and will not even allow us the comfort of a drive in the phaeton or a ride on horseback; we must walk, or engage a public vehicle. Not, my dear reverend mother, that the loss of these luxuries much annoys me, who can never know the use of them in the religious state, but the fact is my chief sadness arises from the fact that I cannot see *you*, or visit our convent as I had hoped. And I do feel very bitterly the unmerited humiliation which is put upon us both by the severity of my father.

"I beg of you, and of all the dear sisterhood, not to forget me in your prayers. I live in hopes of seeing you soon; for who knows, perhaps my father's temper may cool after all. I shall watch anxiously for an answer by return of post if possible; if not, I am sure you will not leave me beyond a day or two; and believe me your very affectionate

"MARION."

"Poor Marion," said Sister Angelique, folding the note, "I must teach you something of the spirit of a Vocation when I *do* write, and that will not be this week. She is ill prepared to face trial. It will not be amiss, should the grace of a Vocation be hers if she meet with a little suffering before she joins us, if indeed her father ever allows her to do so."

"Well, Sister Superior," said the general mistress, an amiable nun of about forty years of age, to whom the management of the young lady pensioners was intrusted, "to judge from appearances, one would not have thought that Marion would have had any wish to engage in our holy state, whilst I *should* have thought it not at all unlikely that, divested of the natural pride of her character, Lilian would one day have been likely to become a

Religious; but does not daily experience prove to us that God calls to His service souls whom one would regard as beings destined for the gay scenes of the world, as well as those who love retirement?"

"Exactly so, Sister Madeleine," replied the Superior; "thus it is that women who have been surrounded with every luxury that wealth can procure, carelessly fling it at the foot of the Cross, and serve God in penance and retirement; whilst those who have been reared in poverty and trial, not unfrequently are in their hearts far more wedded to the world."

A little apart from the group of elder ladies, walked the young nuns, to whom the news that dear Marion Craig was prevented from seeing them had already spread. Some two or three of the sisters had been in the school before their departure to the Novitiate at Namur, and one amongst them had been there at the same time with Marion. In the little world of conventual life, the circumstances attendant on the arrival of a new member, or whatever may occasion that arrival to be delayed, always furnishes some little excitement.

Marion had been prayed for very earnestly and looked for very anxiously by those young people; they often hazarded conjectures as to whether she, in the midst of her father's luxury and opulence, was practising *sub rosa* little austerities which should fit her for those she must constantly practise as a Sister of Notre Dame; for though gentle as to its rule in points of fastings and abstinence, like that of every other religious order, it of course required a spirit of mortification and of perpetual self-abnegation.

That poor Marion did not in the slightest degree possess these qualifications at the present moment, the complaining tone of her letter distinctly shewed; and a compact was entered into between the three youngest nuns to redouble their prayers for her; they declaring that they thought it was owing to their want of fervor that the new sister they had been praying for remained so worldly in her inclinations.

Innocent girls were there, who had made but one step as it were from the well-disciplined school of Canley Heath, to the Novitiate of the mother-house at Namur. Women who had passed perhaps thirty years in the world before they entered religion. Souls who, whatever the world may think or say about the matter, were undoubtedly happy, though they had abjured all that earth holds most dear, in their renunciation of domestic ties, the pleasures of the world, the luxuries which wealth can bestow, and adopted in their place the self-denying life of a nun, with all its austerities, its poverty, its voluntary abandonment of the pleasures of sense, and oh, far, far above all, most painful to human pride, that absolute, that unreserved obedience, by which the religious gives up to the superior the will, that precious will so hard to renounce, so difficult to yield up, and yet the renunciation of which in its full entirety is the first essential in the life of a religious.

Yes, "*He that can receive it let him receive it.*"

It is absurd for the world to maintain that the inmates of cloisters must needs be unhappy because they have abjured the world, or refuse our admiration to that which we ourselves are not called upon to imitate.

But the hour of recreation passes with the fading summer eve, and the sisterhood retire all calm and peaceful as the waning summer day to the convent chapel, and the evening meditation, the examen, and visit to the blessed sacrament close the day, and each one seeks her humble couch, from which she rises in the early morn more refreshed than the woman of the world when she leaves her bed of down.

Leave we the quiet convent, and enter with us a small but neat and pretty house on the Brixton Road, the house of Herbert Leslie, in which dwelt also his mother and sister. A very small but pretty garden surrounds the house, and preparations are being made for the evening meal.

Catherine Leslie, a somewhat plain but very lady-like young woman, sits awaiting the return of her brother. An open letter is in her lap, she has read it over twenty times at least that day. She dearly loved Lilian Craig, and then our Catherine is by no means insensible to the power and influence which wealth bestows. She remembered that if Herbert married Lilian, she would bring him a rich dower, which would enable her poor artist brother to climb a little more quickly up the ladder of life than he could possibly do when his endeavors were thwarted by "poverty's unconquerable bar." Lilian's letter, however, had cast the *Chateaux en Espagne*, which she had been some months building, most ruthlessly to the ground. Her indignation was excited that Herbert, whom she almost idolized for his virtue and his undoubted talent, should be considered unfit to espouse her friend Lilian because he was poor.

At last the long weary day was nearly over, and the hour came at which Herbert generally returned from his studio in Oxford street. Generally Catherine met him with a smiling face; but on this night he saw by the expression of her countenance that something had occurred to disturb her.

She said nothing, but laid the open letter on the table beside the artist's plate.

He perused it in silence, and Kate observed that his fine countenance wore a very sad expression as he laid it on the table.

"I can now understand why Mr. Craig has not answered the letter in which I ventured to solicit the hand of his daughter. Well, then, all hope is over. I dare not bring a woman brought up as Lilian has been, to my own humble house, Kate; nor will I do anything, dearly as I love her, to curtail my sick mother's comforts; but I will see Lilian. Oddly enough, I have to commence next week a painting for the high altar of one of the Preston churches. Preston is but sixteen miles from Lytham, and I will manage to take the train thither; but I will not write—it will be the better way to take Lilian by surprise. Take no notice of her letter, Catherine; this is Thursday, and Monday, the day on which I leave London, will speedily be here."

It was not without reluctance, however, that Kate Leslie agreed to let her friend's letter remain unanswered, for she was one of those persons who always liked to do things in a hurry—no delay where Catherine Leslie was concerned—the word simply did not enter into her vocabulary. When she was a pensioner in the convent school she was *always* in disgrace because she was *always* in a hurry, and consequently things were only half done; quick of apprehension, Kate expected to grasp at an accomplishment whilst others were only thinking about it, to master the difficulties of a language in a few lessons, to play a piece of music through without a mistake, whilst other girls, who had given treble the time to the accomplishment in question, were reading it, thus occasioning endless trouble to the gentle nuns who directed her studies, and endless reprimands, too, for her undue eagerness which ran through, not only her studies, but every occupation of the day.

Catherine was now twenty-four years old, the mistress of her little house, with one tiny servant to direct and govern, a servant who had not numbered more than fifteen years, and consequently was able to do little more than save the delicate hands of her mistress from the performance of the coarser portions of the household work.

Kate knew what it was to do even the rough dirty work, though no one ever saw her with dirty hands or a soiled dress; not a bit of it—she was quite one of the go-a-head sort, was our friend Kate; and when she had dismissed, as she not unfrequently did, "her help," for she could not term her a servant, she would rise at six o'clock, clean and sweep and dust the house down; and be as neat and nice as any lady in the neighborhood by ten o'clock in the morning. Numerous were the squabbles which used to take place between Miss Leslie and her *helps* on the score of their being, as she used to express it, "so terribly slow," that, but for her ill health and her duties as a teacher of German and oil-painting, she would prefer doing all the work herself.

She was scrupulous as to this point of cleanliness; could see dirt and neglect, it will be readily conceived, "her help" either could not or would not see; and yet would be six hours accomplishing what might with ease have been done in two, and only did it by halves after all; and not unfrequently has she been heard to express the unamiable wish that the ladies who used to reprove her at Canley for her undue haste had their tempers tried as hers was by these wretched girls—they would find idleness rather more tiresome to deal with than activity.

Catherine Leslie, however, erred; if, indeed, she did err on the right side; it was certainly no fault of hers if the girls with whom she was plagued, instead of being trained up for domestic service as neat, cleanly, active domestic servants, left her not a whit better than when they came, idle, dirty, and worthless in every sense of the word.

It therefore, as we have already said, did not at all suit her hasty notions to receive a letter from a friend and allow four or five days to pass over without answering it; but as Herbert had expressly forbidden her to do so, there was no help but to submit.

She was, however, but little prepared for the announcement made by Herbert the following morning.

"Catherine," he said, "I can only be absent for a fortnight at the longest; can you make arrangements to enable you to be absent so long from home? if so, come with me to Preston; you are a friend of dear Lilian's, and will call upon her with me."

Of course, such an arrangement was exactly what Kate liked. So promising "her help" a new frock if she attended carefully to her mother in her absence, and mentally resolving to dismiss her on her return home, should she find that household matters had been neglected, Miss Leslie prepared for her expedition into the north with right good will; and on the following Monday morning, they accordingly left the station at Euston Square, having taken their places by second-class for Newton Junction.

CHAPTER V.

A FEW USEFUL HINTS FROM THE CONVENT OF NOTRE DAME—PAPA IS OUTWITTED.

"A LETTER from Canley," exclaimed Marion Craig, as Benson one morning handed her á note, the superscription of which was in the handwriting of the kind old friend who was Sister Superior of the convent, and she eagerly tore it open, whilst Lilian exclaimed—

"One for me, Benson; Kate has treated me shamefully, never answering my letter before; but let me hear the contents of your epistle, Marion, then I will read my own."

"Cheer up, Lilian, dear," replied her sister; "you will find there has been some very good reason for Kate's silence, depend on it. You know *I* must say *mea culpa*, for shame be to me, how I *have* fretted and pined because the nuns have left a letter seven days unanswered. But let me begin," she added, reading her letter aloud. It ran as follows:—

"MY DEAR CHILD,—I was very glad to hear from you, and embrace the first opportunity of replying to your letter.

"Be certain, my dear Marion, that however painful our trials may be they are all ordained for our good; trust to time and, above all, to prayer, and if the Almighty does indeed call you to serve Him in our holy institute, be persuaded that every obstacle will be removed. And should they continue, take it for granted that God has other designs over you; for most assuredly, my dear child, if He has given you a vocation He will also give you the means of following it.

"Rest content, in the quiet country, Marion, as long as it is your father's will, you should remain there. The quietude and calm of the place in which you live will be excellent aids to that inward spirit of recollection which you would do well to keep up, and which *must* be yours should you become a Religious.

"At the same time that you own your compulsory residence in what you term a small cottage, and the privation of your customary use of an equipage, is perhaps well, as it will inure you to the absence of luxuries, and the discomforts of a humble way of living, (although, indeed, the former be not worth mentioning,) yet still, my child, I can see that you are as yet far from possessing that poverty of spirit without which you never will become a true Religious.

"You tell me, too, that you bitterly feel the humiliations your father has put upon you, by depriving you of the use of these luxuries. Ah, my child, accept of these humiliations; fly not from them when they are placed before you. I do not say seek them, Marion, for as yet you cannot bear them when they come unsought for, but learn to recieve them patiently when they do come; for if humility should be the great characteristic of every Christian soul, how much more so that of the Religious; for it forms the very basis of the spiritual life. Regard these little trials as mere nothings, or, at the most, as trifling obstacles thrown in your way in order to test the strength of your Vocation.

"Write to me again shortly; be faithful in all your devotional practices; and receive the little cross of your residence in the country, instead of coming to London, thankfully rather than the reverse. We shall meet each other soon, rely upon it. Believe me, my dear child, your sincere friend, Sister Angelique."

Marion laid down the letter with a deep-drawn sigh. You see this poor young woman still clung marvellously to earth and earthly goods; not much chance, you will say, that she will persevere, if, indeed, she ever enters the Novitiate of Namur. Well, time will show. There are many souls which find their salvation amongst the shoals and quicksands of adversity, perhaps Marion's will be one of these.

Meanwhile Lilian has opened her epistle, and an exclamation of joy escapes her lips, as, on perusing its contents, she finds that Catherine and Herbert are now on their way to Preston.

Her sister's pleasure was not very gratifying to

Marion. Self-love whispers us that it is hard when we think we are harshly dealt by to have our grievances made light of. She could not bear the contrast between her sister's spirits and her own depression, so that she sauntered out on the beach, and choosing a secluded spot, sat down to read, and ruminate, and ponder, over the contents of the letter, till at last she really came to the conclusion she ought to have arrived at long since—namely, that she would follow as faithfully as possible the advice of her friend. Nothing imparts such a charm to the countenance as the consciousness of a heart at ease with itself. Thus Marion was all smiles and cheerfulness, and her always pretty face prettier than usual on her return to the cottage.

It was surely a *fete* day for the two sisters. Mother Angelique's sensible letter, every word full of religion and common sense, had had its effect; and a fervent aspiration had ascended from the depths of that poor proud young heart, so that she felt very resigned and humble, and necessarily very happy.

There was Lilian too, the very picture of good temper, looking so charming in her white muslin robe, and sky-blue ribbons, with Catherine sitting beside her, and Herbert too, the sight of whom would have raised a tempest in Mr. Craig's heart not very easy to be quelled. Marion thought she had never seen her so happy before, yet there was something beneath the surface, and she observed her start and look anxious and uneasy when any person approached the garden gate. There was this difference, you see, between the sisters—Marion was advancing a step or two on the road to virtue, with great difficulty I own, for she went on her way *very* wearily, and though she had put her hand to the plough, she had often turned back ; but poor Lilian had made a retrograde movement ; she had learned her first lesson in deceit that morning, and timid of the consequences, should her father know of the visit of Herbert and his sister, had sent the servant with a note to the Misses Elliot, saying that she was going to be absent from home till evening.

She was enjoying the forbidden fruit ; she had not only corresponded with the Leslies, but was positively entertaining them both for the whole day.

An elegant little dinner was served up for the young ladies and their friends at six o'clock, and they left by the eight o'clock train, Herbert telling the sisters that they should visit them again on the morrow.

"Are you not afraid, Lilian dear, of Catherine and Herbert coming to see us without papa's knowledge?" asked Marion, as they sat together in the quiet moon-light.

"Afraid !" replied Lilian ; "what should I be afraid of? My father will yield his consent to my marriage with Herbert in the end ; and how is he to know that Herbert comes here ? Benson is faithful."

"True, but there are others at Lytham besides Benson. I saw what you did not notice; both Martha and Matilda Elliot were on the beach, walking towards the house near to the old mill when Herbert left us at the garden gate; trust me, Lilian, papa will not be long before he hears of this visit."

"It by no means follows that the Elliots saw or noticed them," replied Lilian: "however, things must take their course; I really feel very indifferent about the matter."

The following Saturday Mr. Craig came as usual to Lytham, and remained until the Monday morning. A great change had taken place, what could it mean? were his dear girls becoming sensible at last, and about to become docile and tractable after all? they were both happy and full of spirits, complained no more of Lytham being dull, called it a beautiful little place, said they should be quite happy for three months or longer, should papa wish them to prolong their stay; and when relenting somewhat, he inquired should he send the phaeton down for them, they both replied in the negative, though from very opposite motives,— Marion because she was now thinking only of denying herself the use of former luxuries, whilst Lilian preferred those quiet but dangerous *tete-a-tetes* with Herbert and his sister.

"What can be the meaning of all this?" he said to himself, as the train steamed out of the station on the following Monday morning. "This conduct is not assumed, the girls are perfectly happy. Well, I suppose it has been always the same since the creation of the world; women *are* incomprehensible creatures, no doubt about it. This removal I had destined as a punishment seems positively turned into a pleasure."

The next morning explained the cause of one at least of his daughters having found Lytham suddenly become as pleasant as it had previously been the reverse.

He received a letter from Miss Elliot; the writer declared herself "shocked beyond conception at the duplicity practised by his daughters towards one of the most indulgent of parents, but she was quite sure that Mr. Craig was not at all aware that Mr. Leslie was in the habit of visiting at Lytham; he had been there, to her certain knowledge, three or four times at the least; this sufficiently explained why Lilian especially had shown herself so averse to her looking after herself and her sister as the writer had promised to do; indeed, she had not been well treated by the studied slights, she might even add, the *intentional* insults, shown her by *both* the young ladies, and should not have troubled herself about them or their indecorous conduct, had she not pledged her word to Mr. Craig to take a friendly interest in his daughters, and become as a mother to them both during their absence from home."

"As the case stood," added the writer, "she felt too much grieved and offended to call at the cottage again, and would merely say that once on the previous week she had received a note from Lilian, breaking an engagement she had made with her, assigning some trivial and doubtless some untrue motive as the cause, and that in the evening herself and her sister had observed Mr. and Miss Leslie leave the cottage; and that on two occasions later they *knew* that the party in question had visited Lilian and Marion in the morning, had remained the whole day, and been seen to leave Lytham by the 8.30 train for Preston in the evening."

"The writer now conceived she had done her duty, and redeemed the promise she had given of watching over his daughters, and felt more grieved at the sorrow she inflicted on mentioning such a dereliction from duty on their part, than angry at the systematic impertinence with which the young ladies had treated herself."

It was part of Mr. Craig's nature to do things without deliberation, therefore he made a very hasty breakfast, Miss Elliot's letter having terribly disturbed him, and took the express train to Lytham, working himself into a fury of anger during his journey. Marion was at the piano, Lilian reading, when their father entered the parlor; for, like all country houses, the hall door could always be opened by merely turning the handle outside, therefore the unsuspecting damsels had no conception that their father was near, till the shoulder of Lilian was seized in his firm grasp, and she was so violently shaken that the book fell from her hand.

A cry of mingled alarm and surprise broke from her lips as, struggling to free herself from that painful grasp, her eyes fell on the enraged countenance of her father.

"Papa, what is the matter? you hurt me," said the terrified Lilian, springing from her seat as soon as he relaxed his hold; whilst Marion gazed timidly, unconscious of the cause of her father's presence there.

"How dare you receive the visits of those Leslies, when I have forbidden you to correspond with them? How dare you presume to encourage the addresses of that beggarly artist?" he exclaimed, now raising his hand to strike, in his anger, the beautiful young woman, who, recovered from her first fright, stood steadily confronting him.

"Herbert has only visited me in company with my old friend Catherine, papa. What harm was there in that? and as to his being poor, there can be no crime in that surely; only a misfortune," replied the undaunted Lilian. "It was yourself who taught me to admire him for the noble qualities he possesses, and"——

"Not another word, not another word; Herbert is making love to *my* pocket, to *my* pocket, do you understand that?" he thundered out, holding her forcibly in her chair,—his tall, stately daughter,—as if she had been a child.

"Let me go, father," said Lilian; "do not treat me like this;" while the terrified Marion, stealing up to her sister's side, exclaimed,—

"Do let Lilian leave the room, papa. I am sure we did not think there was any harm in Herbert and Kate coming here to see us."

"No bandying words with me, for I'll not put up with it from either of you," replied the enraged father, adding, satirically, "and I suppose such a saintly young lady as yourself saw no harm either in your pretty sister's shameful proceedings; of course not. But *I* can understand perfectly well the reason why you both took a sudden fancy to Lytham, you wicked, deceitful girls; but we'll see yet who will be master."

"Father," said Lilian,—by the way, Lilian always used the word father instead of papa when she was angry,—"you are very unjust to us both, to Marion especially. See now, she is far more saintly than poor *I* shall ever be, and you give her no credit for it; here the nuns have been writing, telling her to give up her will, and preaching up patience and resignation, and all that sort of thing, and you are as angry with her as with me, who have never thought of either the one or the other."

"You shall practise both before I have done with you," replied her father, ringing the bell; then turning to his daughters he said, "Tell Benson to put your things together, and get ready to leave Lytham."

And as the sisters left the room they heard the old gentleman tell the servant, who had answered the bell, that her mistress was to make up her bill, as circumstances obliged him to remove his daughters to Manchester immediately.

"That odious, spiteful Miss Elliot has this to answer for," said Lilian; "here is a pretty scene, Marion; I wonder what *will* be the end of it all."

"Have patience, Lilian; do not thwart papa," said the milder Marion; "let all he says pass quietly by, as I have resolved on doing: do not meet violence with violence, for you know how absolutely you depend upon him; and Herbert has no home as yet fit for *you* to share. Nay, promise me, my own Lilian," she added; "he is so fond of us both; in time, I am sure he will relent."

"Relent! yes, I shall believe it when I feel its effects in a little less harsh treatment, Marion. However, I will even follow your advice, which is prompted by religion as well as good sense, and you shall see what a humble, obedient Lilian I will become."

As hastily as, three weeks since, they had been hurried away from their luxurious home in Bowden, so hastily were the sisters dragged from Lytham by their enraged father, only two hours having elapsed from the time of his arrival to that of their departure.

Marion had learned to love the place from the moment that she had fallen into a better frame of mind, and she looked half sorrowfully at the prospect before her, as, leaning on her father's arm, she turned from the cottage gate. It had rained heavily all the morning, but the dry sandy soil scarce showed any vestige of the recent storm. The villas and cottages on the beach looked prettier than ever; and the sunbeams, now stealing through the still hazy atmosphere, shed a golden tint over the distant seas, and lighted up the sails of the old mill.

"Yes, I am sorry to leave Lytham," thought Marion; "for was it not in this quiet spot that I first learned to put in practice the all-important lessons of resignation and humility?"

Go on, Marion; practice makes perfect in the ways of virtue as well as in worldly matters. We prophesy that you will make great improvement in time.

She sighed as she stepped into the railway-carriage, taking a last look at the red brick villas and cottages clustering in the distance, and which an indescribable something told her she would never more behold.

A few moments more, and the peaceful village had vanished from her sight. A litte longer, and she was far from the Fylde district; anon, the tall chimneys and factories of the great commercial town rose again before her eyes, and then, alighting at the railway-station, they found a carriage in readiness to take them on to Bowden.

CHAPTER VI.

POVERTY AND DEATH—A FRIEND IN NEED.

"WHAT is to be done, Catherine? see if your woman's wit can help me in this dilemma," said Herbert to his sister, some two months after the return of Lilian and her sister to Bowden; "this bill must be met, and that immediately; and if I carry four of my paintings to the auction-room, the price at which they would be knocked down will scarcely suffice to pay for the funeral of our poor mother."

Poverty and death, what *can* be worse? yet these united trials had visited the humble dwelling of the Leslies.

Immediately on the return of Catherine from Preston, she had been attacked by typhus fever, but her strong constitution had not succumbed beneath the stroke. She had recovered; but, whilst still languishing under the effects of this severe illness, her mother had caught the fever in its most virulent form, and died in the midst of very distressing circumstances.

Herbert Leslie was a clever, talented man; but it is not always the most clever and talented people that get on the best, for, you see, my dear miss or master, sometimes a very mediocre talent will carry all before it, if there be interest or influence in the background, whilst brighter stars shine unnoticed. Now Herbert had no patronage, you see, so that he worked away during the livelong day in that gloomy studio in Newman Street; and one after another his ideals of the beautiful grew upon the canvas before him and were then consigned to the walls of the Painting Academy, the hanging committee taking especial care to hang them where they would *not* be seen, or else they grew dim and dusty in his own studio, to be finally sold at auction at a price certainly very far from remunerative.

Herbert had been led to imagine, from the interest which Lilian's father had taken in his pursuits when he had become acquainted with him in Manchester some three years since, that he would overlook his own poverty and be content to receive as a son-in-law one whom he had treated as a friend, inviting him to his house, treating him on terms of the closest intimacy; and the sanguine temperament of the young artist had led him to forget the vast disparity existing between riches and poverty. The fact that Mr. Craig, a great connoisseur in works of art, merely patronised him because he had a reverence for talent had never entered the head of this romantic young artist; and he thus presumed to raise his eyes to the beautiful daughter of his host. Visiting at the Laurels frequently, he had been received as one of the family, forgetting that the time would come, and that very shortly, when these day dreams might be all roughly dispelled.

Is it not a pity that talented people live in such a little world of romance of their own creating as really often to be wanting in common sense? Why should Herbert have ventured to suppose that the wealthy millocrat would bestow the hand of his beautiful daughter on a man who had nothing beyond the meagre pittance which his genius could obtain? Lilian had written to him only once after her removal from Lytham: she had shown Mr. Craig the letter, had asked his approval of its contents; it was blistered with her tears, for it informed Herbert that, in obedience to her father's will, all intercourse must cease between them.

The father kissed away her tears, and thanked Heaven that he had two model daughters. Why, the youngest resigns the veil, the holy habit of a religious, the life which shall surely prepare her for an eternity of happiness; the other, one to whom she had given up the affections of her heart, with whom she believes she could tread the thorny path of life happily. Ah, she has her idol, and yet she drags it thence and hurls it from her at your behest!

"Oh, truly, Archibald Craig, yours *are model* daughters!"

"Yes, mine *are model* daughters, friend Gilmour; I repeat the words," said Craig one day, as himself and his friend sat over the wine after those two languid, listless young women had left the table for their own private room. "They have now no will but mine: Lilian—well you know what

Lilian was when I first brought her back to Manchester—how she flung defiance in my face, yet how meekly she submitted after a little more useless rebellion ; and also how her sister has given up her most absurd fancy to become a nun. Trust me, friend Gilmour, if we husbands and fathers had but the moral courage to stand out more firmly, the female part of our households would be better ordered and better governed than they are. See now, had I followed your advice, I had lost both these girls ; and how?—the one married to a beggarly artist like young Leslie ; the other confined, caged up in one of those horrid nunneries, of which"——

"Of which, my good sir, you know absolutely nothing," replied Gilmour ; "but I would ask you one question—Have you never counted on the cost of the forced obedience of your children ? do you not see that there is a forced constraint on each of them ? Why, man, maid Marion is no more the girl she was, nor Lilian either, than black is like to white ; you'll have them both in a decline before long, if you persist in your resolve. Let your girl Lilian have the partner she likes, and my pretty god-daughter the veil ; I should wonder what she could have better. I tell you, as I told you before you sent them to Lytham, that evil will come of it if you thwart them thus—treating grown young women like children indeed !"

"Tut, tut, Gilmour, as I told you before, so I tell you again, leave me to manage my girls my own way. Lilian must and shall have a rich mate, and Marion the same. I know what is best for them; better than they know themselves."

Overawed by the violence of their father, utterly dependent on him, Mr. Craig had indeed had his own way with both of them; and after many fruitless entreaties, and a tearful night, and the destruction by Lilian of some half-dozen epistles, in which affection had peeped out in spite of her fears of him, she had at length penned one which had given him satisfaction. He posted it with his own hands; met Lilian with a smiling face; loaded her with presents and caresses; and dreamed not of the volcano which lay smothering within the depths of her woman's heart.

Nor was Marion less painfully tortured. Neither herself nor Lilian was suffered to lead a retired life, every night beholding them absent from their home. Wherever there was a gay reunion, there Mr. Craig's fair daughters were sure specifically to be put up to the highest bidder. The particular reason for which will be given in our next chapter.

But *revenons a nos moutons*. Times were, you see, very hard with the Leslies; and I should like to know who they are not hard with, when people have their bread to earn by their talents, save, as we have already said, to the happy few who get to the top of the ladder quickly by the help of influence and interest rather than by genius. Never were times surely darker than those in which the brother and sister sat talking of the *dismal thing* above. No longer of themselves, for the casket, with its still pale face, alone remained; they were conversing of those sad topics, always sad, far more sad, too, if the survivors are poor. They have but a solitary five-shilling-piece in the house; how shall they pay the undertaker? how shall they pay for their mourning? or for the last quiet home with the remains of her husband in the cemetery at Norwood? Yet there are many who would gladly comply with this work of mercy, and bury the dead, did they know of that distressing case.

The Leslies, however, knew but few persons, and to these they could not apply; for if they had the will, they lacked the power to help them.

Catherine had sat for some moments weeping silently, and Herbert still pursued his walk, with folded arms and moody brow, up and down that little parlor, when his sister suddenly arose, and with a feeble step approached him. She had resolved to mention a name he had forbidden her to utter—a name the faithful friend had not breathed, save in her prayers, for many a weary month—a name which Herbert, she well knew, fondly cherished still.

She was so weak that she had to hold by the table as she attempted to cross the room; but her brother, utterly lost in his gloomy reverie, noticed her not till her light touch fell upon his arm.

"Catherine, my love," he said, "why do you leave the couch?"

She fixed her big dark eyes on his face, and uttered the one word, "Lilian."

"Lilian! what of her, Catherine? Don't rake up old sorrows, dear; we have enough, Heaven knows, to bear without that."

"Lilian would help us, Herbert," still pleaded the fair speaker.

"No more of this, Catherine; I cannot bear it," he exclaimed, darting from her as if stung by a viper. "Lilian! the *false* Lilian, help to put my poor mother in the grave! Never, never! Catherine, I'll sell half the house contains first."

Catherine tottered to the couch, but she still pleaded for the absent Lilian.

"Lilian is true as ever. Lilian is forced to do the will of her despotic old father. I would pledge my life upon her truth."

"Why has she ceased to correspond with you?"

"Why? because she dare not; do you not think her letters would be intercepted? Lilian false! Lilian untrue! Never, never! As soon would I believe the moon would fall from the heavens, as waver for one moment in my faith in Lilian's truth."

All the woman's earnest soul spoke out in these few words. Herbert approached her, and said very sorrowfully,—

"It is not the remains of a mere school-girl's intimacy which can make *you*, with your sound, clear good sense, speak and think so highly of my lost Lilian. Tell me, Catherine, why is it you steadily persevere in thinking so well of one of whom I have such just cause for complaint."

"Because I know Lilian to be a true-hearted, constant woman," she replied; "one whose nature is too noble to allow her to be false where she has pledged her word. There is even something to admire in her very pride, if I may dare so to speak, for it makes her shrink with horror from an untruth; and sure am I she has not broken her faith with you. Remember in the one short note I received from her at the time she intimated to you her obedience to her father's will, she implored us both to wait the result of time, adding, 'The time will come, Catherine, when you will see that I am not untrue.' Let *me* write to her, Herbert; she will help us in our deep distress, and you will find her your own faithful Lilian still."

It was not without considerable reluctance on the part of Herbert that he acceded to his sister's wish, and it was finally settled that the note, written by his sister, should be posted from London, Lilian having many friends in the metropolis, lest the letter, falling by chance into the hands of Mr. Craig, and bearing the Brixton postmark, should awaken his jealous fears.

Very slowly the hours passed away till the morning of the second day brought the answer.

"There is an enclosure," said Catherine, as with trembling fingers she broke open the seal.

Three bank-notes, each for ten pounds, were folded within a sheet of notepaper. Catherine and

Herbert had anxiously looked for a note. It contained only these few words—

"From your faithful and affectionate
"LILIAN."

That thirty pounds was all the world to the Leslies, but the load still lay heavily at the heart of Herbert. Meanwhile, directions were given for the funeral, good mourning was purchased, and there was still money in hand.

The Leslies little knew how it fared with Lilian just then, or how she, the daughter of the wealthy Mr. Craig, had procured the thirty pounds.

Let us go back a little, and show in the next chapter how things were going on at the Hollies.

CHAPTER VII.

HOW, AND FOR WHAT PURPOSE, LILIAN PARTED WITH HER BRACELET.

LILIAN and Marion are alone.

"What a wonder to be alone! it *is* a relief to be one evening to ourselves," said the younger of the two, as she bathed her fevered temples, fevered from late hours and dissipation. "I really think I shall die under it, Lilian dear, if papa continues to drag us into company like this; and the worst of it all is that we can no longer be blind to the reason why he hurries us into society. The day of strife must come after all," she added, with a deep sigh; "I dread it too. Heaven grant we may not be found wanting."

"Yes, Marion," answered the still beautiful Lilian; "and *I* dread also this most unnatural strife, this offering us as it were to the highest bidder; nor is it possible to fail at surmising the cause. The last interview with my father, when he informed me that some little time hence we might be the tenants of a very poor home, unless the wives of the rich mill-owners, Messrs. Hartly and Arnold, let me into a little of the truth; but welcome poverty, with all its horrors, my Marion, rather than the gilded miseries of nuptials where hands, but not hearts, are yoked together."

"Ay, my Lilian, you speak right well," said Marion; "and I say too, welcome poverty, a thousand times welcome, rather than be untrue and false to one's vocation. No; in obedience to him, I have led a dissipated life, when my heart has been far away in scenes of cloistered quiet, for *I* have never loved, my sister; but sure there cannot be a greater sin than to wed unloving, above all, to wed when God has called one to serve Him in religion."

"Speak low, Marion," said her sister; "I thought I heard some one near the door. We have both refused the addresses paid to us, and my father's violence terrifies me beyond expression; but I fancy there will soon be an end of this persecution, perhaps sooner than either of us imagine."

As Lilian ceased speaking the door opened, and a servant appeared with a letter; he said, "For Miss Craig."

It was the note written by our friend Catherine. Lilian recognized the handwriting. Lilian— faithful, loving, but misjudged Lilian—positively pressed the inanimate paper to her lips. Do not let us laugh at her for her folly, for how many of us have done the same when some dearly-loved absent friend's letter has fallen within our grasp.

Large tears fell from the eyes of the sisters as they perused Catherine's letter.

"Not a word about Herbert," sighed Lilian;

"but Catherine is right—discreet, prudent Catherine."

"What is to be done, Lilian?" said Marion. "Papa keeps us cruelly short of money; and the worst of it is the idea we now have that his resources are really cramped make it impossible for us to ask him; besides, he would want to know what we require it for; and I don't think less than ten pounds would be of any service; do you, Lilian?"

"Ten pounds, Marion! I cannot send a farthing less than twenty, love; nay, I would send fifty if I had it. There will be poor Mrs. Leslie's funeral to pay for, and mourning for Catherine and dear Herbert—Herbert I mean," she said, as if the use of that little epithet had broken the compact she had made with her own heart. "Come with me, Marion, love; let me see how I can manage."

Lilian entered her bedroom, locked the door, and then opened her jewel-box: she looked wistfully at a diamond necklace, took it up, then replaced it, saying, "Papa would miss that, should he drag us out to-morrow night." Then she took a diamond bracelet, carefully wrapped it up, and laid it aside. "That will do," she said; "papa gave eighty guineas for it. I shall wrap myself in a large mantle, and as soon as he has taken his afternoon's nap, I shall find my way to Silver, the jeweller's, a little way out of Manchester, and see if I cannot get, or raise, twenty pounds on it."

"O Lilian, Lilian, take care," responded Marion.

"What a scene my father will make, if he finds you are parting with your trinkets ; besides, Lilian, you may be seen, and a pretty thing it will be to get abroad that Mr. Craig's daughters are raising money on their jewels."

"Nonsense, Marion, you shall help me to dress up," said her sister. "Come, help me at once," she said, opening a press, from which she took a dark dress and a large mantle, the folds of which enveloped and thoroughly disguised her stately and elegant form ; then she put on a close cottage bonnet, with a veil of black lisse gauze, and the disguise of Lilian to any but a close observer was complete.

Vainly did Marion beg her sister to allow her to accompany her—Lilian was obstinate ; and seizing the opportunity when the servants were not in the way, and amid the twilight of the lovely autumnal evening, Lilian sallied from her home.

Arrived in Manchester, the daughter of the man who was deemed worth thousands of pounds stole like some guilty thing down a street in which she knew a rich jeweler and money-lender resided, and passing the open shop she entered a doorway on which was the inscription—"Private office for reception of valuable property."

Overcoming the natural repugnance she felt to the task she had so nobly taken on herself, Lilian pushed open the door, which gave ingress to a small and well-lighted room at the back of the shop. Her heart beat violently at the novelty of her position: the previous night she had been the belle at a ball given by one of the principal families in the county; that evening she stood humbly attired in the office of a pawnbroker, waiting to raise money on the bracelet which so very lately had glistened on her arm—quietly awaiting the pleasure of the jeweller to serve her. She was engaged in an act of mercy; and, verily, bravehearted Lilian, thou shalt not lose thy reward. After the lapse of a few minutes the master of the shop approached, requested her to be seated, and attentively examined the precious bauble she placed in his hand.

"Thirty guineas you require, madam, on this bracelet?" he said. "The wife or daughter of one of our millocrats is the owner, I'll be bound; some extravagant bill to pay, I suppose, which father or husband must not know of." Such were his thoughts as he minutely examined the trinket.

"Can you lend me the sum required?" stammered forth Lilian.

"Oh yes, certainly," replied Mr. Silver. "The name, if you please," he added, drawing out a sheet of card-board, from which he tore off two tickets, intending one to be attached to the bracelet and the duplicate for the disguised lady before him. Now Lilian was, we need hardly say, entirely a stranger to the mode of proceeding adopted by those who are driven to so painful an expedient as to raise money on their property.

"Name! what name?" said Lilian, mechanically; she really knew not what she said.

"You are not used to raise money in such a way, madam," said the pawnbroker, in a more respectful tone of voice than that which he had previously used, "or you would be aware that the name and address of the person to whom the property belongs is by law obliged to be given to him who lends the money."

Lilian's cheeks glowed like a coal of fire as the name of Craig fell from her lips. Mr. Silver started, but instantly recovered himself.

"Excuse me, madam, the Christian name also," he said.

"Elizabeth," said Lilian, promptly, remembering that Lilian was uncommon, and wishing still to preserve her incognito if possible.

"Your residence?"

"The Laurels, Altrincham." The pawnbroker bowed, placed the duplicate in Lilian's trembling hand, and counted out ten sovereigns in gold, which he tendered to her with two ten-pound notes.

Not once had she raised the veil which had covered her beautiful, tearful face; now she gathered her mantle closely around her, and having carefully deposited the money in a portmonnaie, she returned the "good evening" of Mr. Silver, and hurried from his shop. Silver stood for perhaps the space of two or three minutes blankly gazing at the door through which she had departed.

"Strange," he said; "very strange; there will surely be a hideous crash up at the Hollies. I knew the bracelet again directly—could swear to it amidst a thousand; I repaired it only a few months since, when one of the clasps was broken. Then again, a few nights back came those silver dishes; I am certain they were Craig's property. If I mistake not, my late visitor was one of those beautiful daughters of his who have run away with many hearts and not lost their own. I could swear to the owner of the bracelet, even had she not involuntarily given me her name." Meanwhile Lilian, brave Lilian, threaded her way with rapid step back to her father's dwelling, and also did a deed of charity ere she reached her home to one of the poor cottagers, and thus was able to avert the curiosity of the hall porter who admitted her, by asking the question,—

"Has my father or sister expressed alarm at my absence, Robert? I have been to see poor widow Whiteside, and am home later than I intended."

The man answered in the negative, and Lilian hurried up to her sister's room, threw her arms around her neck, and opening her purse displayed its contents.

Sweet Lilian Craig, your tears of shame are now exchanged for tears of joy, for you feel the exquisite pleasure of doing good to those you love.

Ah, Lilian and Marion, brave and true-hearted heroines of domestic life, both true to your respective vocations, but patiently biding thy time, be it mine to tell how like burnished gold thou didst both come forth from the fiery furnace of tribulation pure and unscathed, truer, far truer and more faithful than in the sunny days of prosperity.

CHAPTER VIII.

THE BANKRUPT MERCHANT.—FAITHFUL AND TRUE.

THE following morning Lilian and her sister sat alone in the library. They were reading; but the thoughts of Lilian were far away, for she knew that the following day was that appointed for the funeral of her good old friend Mrs. Leslie. For some time past the murmur of voices in the adjoining room had been distinctly audible; but her attention had not been attracted, for she knew that her father alone used the apartment opening from the library, and was not aware that the door was ajar.

Suddenly, however, Marion arose from her chair, and with parted lips, and a countenance colorless as marble, stood beside her sister; one hand raised to her lips, to enjoin silence, and the other pointing to the door.

At a loss to comprehend her meaning, and startled at the terrible change in her sister, Lilian was about to rise, but Marion held her down, and bending forwards whispered the one word "Listen!"

"Ruin, absolute and immediate ruin, and no hope of averting it even for a few short months; is that what you mean?"

Slowly and deliberately these words had fallen from the lips of Mr. Craig, and they fell like an icebolt on the hearts of his daughters.

"Exactly so, Mr. Craig," replied his visitor, and Lilian recognized the voice as that of her father's solicitor, whose visits had been very frequent lately, "exactly so ; your unhappy mining speculations, which have turned out so miserably, of themselves were sufficient to drag you into frightful distress ; and at the back of them comes this frightful panic in the cotton-market, which will in the end ruin many whose fortunes are as firm to-day as yours unhappily are the reverse. You will not be able to meet a hundredth part of the liabilities now falling upon you. You must declare yourself bankrupt, Mr. Craig, and get it over as quickly as possible. The sooner the better."

"Bankrupt, bankrupt!" Lilian heard her unfortunate father murmur ; "has it, then, come to this? My God! what will become of me in my old age, and of my self-willed foolish girls?"

"Did you not tell me, sir, that two of the wealthiest of the Manchester gentry, large landed proprietors, as well as mill-owners, had paid their addresses to your beautiful and accomplished daughters? Did you not say you should push on these marriages as speedily as possible?"

"Exactly so, Mr. Hedley ; and for the best of all possible reasons. - Hartly is much attached to Lilian ; Arnold not less so to my daughter Marion. Arnold is more open-handed than the other ; but of course, if once these girls were their wives, circumstances would be much altered. Not only would there be a splendid establishment for each of them, but they would be both off my hands, and the horrors now impending over me be averted, perhaps even entirely prevented. Arnold knows something of my difficulties. He is very fond of Marion; pursues her all the more vehemently the more she slights him, and has told me he will advance me a large sum the moment the wedding-day is fixed."

"And were I in your place, Mr. Craig," replied the lawyer, "that day should be one in the following week at latest. You know the old maxim, my dear sir,—'Self-preservation is the first law of nature.' You may save yourself by marrying your daughters to these men; the result will be a few tears no doubt, perhaps a fit of hysterics, and the other pretty little arts which are generally resorted to by the fair sex; but in the end they will become happy and contented wives, and grateful to you for having found them rich and good husbands. But you told me Miss Marion had some mad notion in her head about becoming a nun; you have not let Arnold into this vagary, I hope? Men are not fond of marrying devotees, you know."

"All right as to that," replied Mr. Craig; "I have forbidden Marion to mention her silly wish to any one. But these girls are harder to manage, Hedley, than you think; for here is one of them not heart-whole, and the other pining after convent fancies. If my only hope rests on the obedience of my rebellious daughters, I really see nothing but the immediate ruin you spoke of when we began to talk of the terrible state of my affairs."

"Excuse me, Mr. Craig," said the lawyer, "but really I think you *are* wanting in firmness; you should *insist* on your children giving up such nonsensical fancies. I know Arnold well; he is just the man to wait long and patiently for your daughter, and punish her for slighting his addresses when he has her in his power; take my advice now,—'Strike the iron while it is hot;' have your own way for once in your life, and save yourself at all events."

"I will see them both, Hedley, and do my best with them, depend on it," replied Craig, rising and walking with his visitor to the door, which gave egress to the hall.

"And do not rest content with *asking* them if they will marry these men; tell them that you have made up your mind that they *shall* do so," were the last words of the lawyer as he quitted the room.

Now, a very pretty piece of dumb show had been acted in the library, by one at least of the young ladies, whose future was being so summarily disposed of. Lilian had twice started to her feet; whilst Marion—especially when the lawyer had urged her father utterly to disregard her own wishes and force her into marriage—had then impotently clenched her little fist, and shook it in the air in the direction whence the voice proceeded. It was well, too, that the ladies wore muslin robes, for the slightest rustle of a silk dress would inevitably have announced their presence.

At first Lilian felt inclined to rush into her father's presence, but, on second thoughts, she decided on seeking her own room, and giving a few hours for thought and reflection; a wise resolve, which she was not, however, to put into execution, for the next moment the heavy tread of her father was heard advancing to the library. To retreat was impossible. They exchanged a significant glance, and still maintained the same attitude.

Mr. Craig's look of mute surprise, as he observed *who* were the tenants of the library, was exchanged for one of indignation; for the very position of the sisters told him they had been listening to all that had passed.

"A praiseworthy, honorable employment, young ladies," he remarked satirically; "however, it has saved me the pain of telling you both that I am a ruined man; that my safety rests with *you;* and that for your own sakes, if not for mine, you must not,—nay, shall not trifle with the overtures for an honorable settlement in life, which has been offered to both of you."

Tears rushed to the eyes of each, but Lilian dashed them impatiently aside; she had not forgotten what that odious lawyer had said about the pretty little arts of womankind, and exclaimed,—

"You will find me willing to endure any hardships poverty may entail, my father; but the day will *never* come in which Lilian Craig will sell herself, or endure to be sold, for gold."

"Amiable, gentle, self-sacrificing Lilian," replied her father, with the greatest calmness and deliberation, "you are what I but *expected* I should find you. And what do you say, Marion?—but stop, not one word yet," he continued; "I wish you to count up the cost of rebellion to my wishes, of clinging to your foolish fancy. Now, in the first place, as you have been playing the eavesdropper, you have of course learnt that I am, as I have just told you,—a ruined man. As things stand at the present moment, that there is no fortune for either of you to look to, whether it be to enrich a needy husband or a cloister of nuns; that a life of privations, the horrors of which you, who have been reared in luxury, cannot tell till you come to know them, await you; whilst, on the other hand, you will live in the ease and affluence you have always enjoyed, with those who are content to take you, doubtless, as you will now be; and at the same time, if there be a spark of filial love left within your bosoms, it may perhaps warm into something of life, if I remind you that by doing this you not only secure your own happiness, but smooth the last years of your aged parent; for, my daughters," said Mr. Craig, rising from his seat, "my utter ruin, or the bolstering up of my tottering fortune rests with you."

A perceptible shudder shook the frame of each of his unhappy children, as Mr. Craig thus alluded to the most painful part of the conversation they had overheard.

The sisters had known him only as a fond and over-indulgent parent till within the last two years, and they had been acute enough to feel convinced that the key to his seemingly eccentric and harsh conduct lay in his desire to see them established in the same way of life in which they had always moved, and at the same time save himself by their means from the ruin impending over him in consequence of his own rash and ill-directed mismanagement of his once large income.

One after another rose before the eyes of the unhappy Lilian and her sister a thousand little acts of parental love and fond indulgence, whilst before them pleaded—ah, would that we could say with dignity—the white-headed father, who was content to sacrifice the years of their youth and maturity for the short span which might yet remain to him of life.

Lilian paced up and down the library; she asked herself, "Would Christian saint or Spartan hero demand such a sacrifice?" and her keen perception of right and wrong replied with an unhesitating "No."

She paused before him in her weary walk. "My father," she said, "I will not forsake you; your Lilian has accomplishments and talents she can place to good account. Fear not—*I* do not fear,—but ask me not to wed for the love of gold."

"As I expected, Lilian," he calmly replied; then turning to his youngest and best-loved daughter, he added, "and what is your determination, Marion?"

"To give up for the present, for the discharge of a filial duty, the desire which I feel to leave the world,—to work for you, live for you, die for you, if needs be, my father; but ask me not, tempt me not, to break this my resolve. Would that I could do your will, and save you from impending ruin—but this I cannot avert."

"Enough, enough, my children," said the old man, hastily rising; and waving his hand impatiently, he dashed past them to the solitude of his own chamber. He spent therein two weary hours communing with his own sad thoughts. He felt convinced that expostulation and entreaty were alike useless; for could he—dared he—drag them to the altar in defiance of all rights, human and divine?

It was late in the evening ere he could bear to seek their company. They sat alone, silent and sorrowful, in the elegant boudoir in which they had passed so many happy hours.

Perhaps adversity would, after all, be beneficial to that poor worldly heart: he was certainly in a softer mood than was his wont. He approached them both.

"You have sorely grieved me, girls," he said, "thus to run counter to my wishes, and that just now when ruin presses heavily upon me; ay, and your beauty too would have placed you high amongst the matrons of our city. But let it be, let it be,— we will tread the rough paths of life then, as we have glided down the smooth ones, together; but, alas, alas, my Marion and Lilian, you know not how thorny will be the future which spreads before us!"

CHAPTER IX.

THE SHADY SIDE OF LIFE—IMPORTANT NEWS: STRANGE, IF TRUE.

"WHEN will she come back—when will she come back?" murmured, in a querulous tone of voice, an aged, imbecile man, as he drew aside the curtain which shaded the first-floor window of a small house in one of the network of streets which run between the Walworth Road and Kennington Common, or Park, as it is now termed.

The night was dark and gloomy, black clouds flitted across the starless sky, and a drizzling rain pattered against the window. Archibald Craig moved from the window with a heavy heart; his fortunes, and those of his children, were gloomy as was the November night.

Oh, what a contrast between that poor abode in the small seven-roomed house in the Palmerston Road, and Mr. Craig's former stately abode at Bowden! Two years have passed away; the break up is spoken of as a thing of the past; Marion and Lilian, the belles of the county in which they lived, are now two poor young ladies, enduring that— what shall we call it—well, that severest of *all* distress, the distress of the well educated and the gently born.

Who thinks now of Marion? The poor daily governess, who leaves home early in the morning, in her simple gray merino dress and cloth mantle, to wile away the weary, weary day, how weary those alone know who are cooped up the livelong day with high-spirited and sometimes ill-tempered children, and then returns, long after the shades of night have fallen, not even to meet a bright face and sunny smile, but whose task it then is to soothe the querulousness of old age; and when she lays her aching head upon the pillow, before she sleeps she will bedew it with her tears, because she knows not how to eke out her slender pittance. Who cares now for Marion? Who cares now for Lilian? the stately queen-like Lilian, beautiful and accomplished as she is?—but she is only the wife of Herbert Leslie the poet-painter. They married and reckoned without their host, when they thought they would do well in the world; things seemed at the fairest merely to entrap them as it were into matrimony; it is the shady side of life with them. Who cares now for Lilian?

"*Vanite des vanites; et tout est vanite!*"

Well, but we wander from our point. We are not going to tell you of Lilian just now, but of Marion, the self-devoted daughter, who practises an act of heroic virtue every day and hour of her life.

On, on through blinding sleet and cold gusts of wind, along the open Clapham Road does she thread her way with rapid step. It is a wretched night for that delicate young woman, used as she has been to every luxury, fenced in in her happy girlhood, lest the breeze of heaven should blow too roughly upon her, to tramp along that lone dark road, for it is past nine at night; but, you see, when she left home in the morning there was just one shilling in the house; she could not spend it in riding, it would purchase a humble meal at night. O reader, try and realise to yourself the misery of not having a pound in the whole world, and not knowing how to get it, and if you have not been soft-hearted all your life to others, you will surely begin to be so now. On still, a long walk of one hour and a half before you can reach your home. A weary pilgrimage is thine, poor Marion.

Marion had visited the Canley Heath Convent that day. Why was she happy amidst all her sharp sorrow? Why, because Sister Angelique had drawn aside from the boisterous pupils who had accompanied her hither, had spoken words of gentle loving-kindness, had reminded her,—ah, who more likely to do so than holy priest and gentle nun?—whatever the world may say, that surely she was doing the will of God, in staying in the world to support and care for him who, imbecile and helpless, could not help himself; and thus had ended her speech:—

"Remember, my child, your loss of fortune makes no difference to us. When by the death of your father you shall be free, the Novitiate of Namur will be open to you; and the Community of Notre Dame, should you make your vows as a religious, will receive you without a pension."

"Alas! my good mother, I shall indeed have nothing to bring you now, nothing save a good will, good health, a good education; and ah, I had almost forgotten something else," she added, smiling archly, and holding up her small white hands. "You know you have no lay sisters or servants in your Institute of Notre Dame, and I shall be able to do lots of work with these little hands of mine."

"Ah, we shall see, we shall see," said the Sister Superior, laughing. "I do not think they look as if they had done much hard coarse work as yet, Marion; perhaps you may be put in the school, you know."

"Well, then, I can teach French and German, and painting and music, and half-a-dozen other things beside," said Marion, laughing; "but I fancy these hands of mine do rather more than you give them credit for. Do you know, dear Sister Superior, they light the fire every morning, sweep the room, and do half-a-dozen other things? only, I of course plead guilty to the vanity of wearing gloves in order to keep them white."

"Very right, my dear child," rejoined the Superior; "you are in the world, and teaching as a governess, your little pupils would soon lose their respect for you, Marion, did they behold you with the red, coarse hands of one who does a servant's hard work."

This little conversation with the good Sister Superior had sent Marion on her way rejoicing; she must bear *the burden of the day and its heats* for an indefinite period, it was true, but still there was a haven of rest at last. She would go on caring for and helping him to whom she was all the world; and then,—yes, *then*,—when her work for him was over, she could bring her trim little bark into the harbor of religion.

It was half-past nine that stormy November night before she reached the house in which she lodged; wet, weary, and fatigued, she ascended the staircase. Her father, now imbecile, and always more or less querulous, had worn himself out with pacing up and down the narrow limits of his little room, imagining to himself a thousand horrors about Marion. He would have it she had been garroted, or run over in that long dark road; and as his watch and he had long since parted company, had worn out his landlady with inquiries, repeated certainly every ten minutes, as to the time.

"My dear child, you have frightened me out of my wits. What *can* have detained you so long?" he said, as Marion entered the room.

"I am not much later than usual, papa," said Marion, forcing a smile, and throwing off her cloak, which was wet through; "but time hangs heavy on your hands; you have nothing to do, you see, so grow timid and apprehensive about me."

"Not without a cause, not without a cause," murmured the old man, with a sigh; "as to myself,

Marion, I read till I can read no longer, and then I amuse myself with sitting at the window and watching my neighbors. How true it is, my dear, that one-half the world know not how the other half live. I could never have imagined, when I was revelling in luxury at Bowden, that positively genteel people herded together as they do in this very street; for instance, why, my dear, these are only six-roomed houses, and positively there are three families living in one of them opposite; first, the people who own the house,—I have ascertained without a doubt that they are located in the lower apartments, or kitchens, to speak properly,—then the shabby-genteel people, as we call them, have the parlors, and up-stairs there are those pale, ladylike young women whom we see perpetually embroidering at the windows; and then I set to work reckoning up what the mechanic and his wife, who hold the house, may make by letting the whole of it in furnished rooms, especially if they are furnished like these."

Marion cast a contemptuous glance around the room, mentally calculating for how much she could purchase the sordid furniture it contained.

It was a fair specimen of a third-class London lodging-house, this small suburban residence; for Marion's first-floor room had apologies for curtains, an old settee dignified by the name of a couch, an uneasy, rather than an easy chair, with a tall, straight back and ponderous arms, an old-fashioned piano of the spinet class, a dingy, well-worn drugget, four cane chairs with green baize carefully nailed over the worn seats, whilst in the bedroom a piece of wood nailed against the window-sill did duty as a toilet-table. Mrs. Shears, the landlady, had no notion of putting good articles into her lodger's rooms—no, not she,—they were sure to spoil them, she was wont to say; any makeshift did for lodgers. Thus, by charging a good price for the use of her worn-out furniture, and by sundry other peculations, she and her husband managed pretty well to live out of their small house and the two sets of lodgers, and the single gentleman who dwelt therein.

Marion was yet lingering over a warm cup of tea the old gentleman had made for her, when the postman's double knock caused her to hurry to the door.

She heard the man pronounce her name, and hastening down-stairs she received a lady's dainty epistle, also another in a large blue envelope, such as commercial gentlemen generally use. Trembling with agitation she re-entered the room, and first breaking the seal of the tiny little perfumed note, she read as follows:—

"Mrs. Burke is desirous to engage the services of an English lady as daily governess. Her daughter, recently returned from Canley Convent, informs her that Miss Craig will shortly be disengaged. Mrs. Burke will pay one hundred pounds a year, and will require Miss Craig's services five hours daily. She will be glad of an early answer."

The letter fell from Marion's hands. "A hundred a year!" she exclaimed; "but it is in Ireland, such a way from dear Canley Convent. However, it cannot be helped. O papa, think how delightful to be engaged only for five hours, to have all my long evenings at home, and get just as much again as I am having now."

"You have forgotten your other letter, Marion," said her father; "but dear me, child, it looks like a lawyer's letter," he added, placing the letter in her lap.

"Oh, I can't bear to see these large blue letters!" said Marion, pushing it aside: "I really feel afraid to open it;" then turning it over and examining the postmark, she exclaimed,—

"Why, it is positively from Manchester; and see, papa, the handwriting is that of dear, good Mr. Gilmour;" then breaking the seal, Marion read as follows:—

"MY DEAR MARION,—I think it well that you should hear of something which may tend to raise your spirits in this your day of trial; so I will tell you the good news which I have heard about you in a very odd manner. I happened to call in at Heywood's, the law-stationer, in the High Street yesterday, and his head clerk let me into a very great secret about yourself. He said he had been engrossing the will of a lady of rank, to whom Miss Craig was well known; and that her name was down for a legacy, amongst various bequests to other persons, for no less a sum than two thousand pounds! Now, my dear Marion, this lady cannot possibly be any other than your late most kind friend the Dowager Lady Evelyn. She is both aged and infirm in health; what more likely than that she should have drawn up her will at this very time, and should remember by a bequest one whom she has so nobly assisted in life? I could not get him to confide to me the name of the lady in question; indeed, he seemed half in fear after he had opened his mind, saying, that it would be considered a scandalous breach of confidence, which would cost him his place were it made known. Keep up your spirits then, your past and your present forlorn position is well known; and so many things point out Lady Evelyn as being the party alluded to, that I myself have no doubt as to who the angel in human shape is who has determined one day to rob your path of its thorns. She has taken a great interest in you. She is a woman of large fortune, childless, and a widow; so hope on, and keep up your courage.—With kind remembrances to Mr. Craig, I am, dear Marion, your sincere friend,

"JOHN GILMOUR."

The letter fell from Marion's hands. She was dazed, bewildered; she knew not what to think; she was inclined to be incredulous.

"Would Lady Evelyn ever bear *me* in such kindly remembrance, and yet not cheer my troubled path by telling me that my future, so dark and so uncertain now, had been thus kindly cared for?" was the first question she put to the sanguine old man, who, three short years since, would have held the sum reported to be left to his daughter in Lady Evelyn's will as of very small consequence indeed.

"I do not see that her silence to yourself has anything at all to do in the matter," urged the old gentleman, somewhat displeased with Marion's incredulity; "but it is always the way with you. Do you not see that she might fear that this should become public. No person ever liked the dispositions of their will to be made known during their lifetime. Besides, Marion, remember *how* her ladyship has addressed you."

"Yes, quite true," replied Marion; and a bright gleam shot across her features as she replied, "true, papa, human kindness cannot surpass hers: think with what delicacy she sent me a check for a hundred pounds, when your bankruptcy had taken place; and then later, how we have often profited by her benevolence. Only a few days since, too, remember how she wrote me, saying, 'she had kept silence so long that she feared lest her own sufferings made her selfish, and neglectful of me.' It was very strong language to use," she continued, after a pause. "What if she did seem neglectful of me? what if she really *were* so? *I* had surely no right to complain."

"None whatever," replied her father; "but the very familiarity of her intercourse strengthens the idea in which we are led to indulge."

"Yes," replied Marion, "if true; and without some foundation, how should such a story have reached Mr. Gilmour's ears?"

Thus the conversation terminated. And Marion went to bed, reproaching herself that ever and again she found her thoughts reverting to this strange story, thinking how happy she might make the last days of her father if it were true; and then blaming herself for letting her thoughts thus run riot, for she remembered that the death of a kind friend must inevitably take place before this story, strange, if true, could be verified in her regard.

CHAPTER X.

THE WAY TO MAKE HOME HAPPY—THE SHADOW OF DEATH.

"LILIAN dear, I think I shall leave you very soon," said Catherine Leslie, one winter afternoon, as, supported by pillows, she played with the tiny hands of an infant, some three months old, which lay in Lilian's lap.

"Nay, Catherine dear, do not speak so," replied Lilian; "you have been better, much better lately, spite of the winter weather. If things take a turn for the better, we may all be so happy together; indeed, no blow would be heavier to me than that of your death, always excepting that of my doting sister."

"But it *will* come nevertheless, Lilian, and perhaps at the moment when we least expect it," said Catherine. "I am convinced that the change for the better which I really feel is a mere delusion; for myself, I have not a wish for my life to be prolonged. My sole desire on earth is that I could see the dawn of brighter days for you."

"No more of this, love; you make me feel quite sad," said Lilian. "I owe so much to you, Catherine, that I cannot bear to think that the day is perhaps very near in which we must part."

"Owe so much to *me*, Lilian," replied the humble Catherine, with a slight laugh. "I wonder what Lilian could learn of me."

"The art of making a home happy, Catherine; of husbanding my humble means; of keeping it neat and in good order; of making my own dresses, pies and puddings, cooking a dinner; and last, though not least, you have taught me so well the practice of economy that I can positively make one shilling go as far as five when I first strove, as Mrs. Leslie, to keep house myself."

"Ah, Lilian, but you were an apt and a docile pupil too," said Catherine; "you did not resent, as some would have done in your place, my offer of showing you how to manage your little home; and after all, dearest, how very little *could* I do."

"How very *little?* rather say how very *much*," said Lilian; "for, Catherine, these very *little duties* of everyday life, *so* little that our sex are too apt to pass them by as beneath their notice, comprise in their fulfilment the very essence of domestic happiness; in their neglect, the misery of the whole household."

Lilian spoke but too truly; she was the light of her own home, humble though it was; plunged from the highest affluence to poverty, she had had much to learn. Very weary and repulsive was the task at the beginning, but she had put her hand to the plough, and would not look back. Reason, love, and religion came to her aid. Brave Lilian, the slatternly wife of the mechanic, with double the money earned by your poor author and artist husband, Herbert, might look at you and learn a lesson for the future.

Industrious Lilian, the wife of the man with his hundred and fifty pounds or two hundred a year, may come and learn of you how to keep her house in order, and make her husband love his home; for you would teach her that the thorough discharge of the duties of domestic life are not incompatible with the tastes of a refined and intellectual mind, should a reverse have plunged such a one from affluence into comparative poverty.

When Lilian first essayed the art of housekeeping she made such sad blunders that she turned to the experienced but sensitive Catherine for her lesson. It was not very long before it was well learnt, and Lilian's white hands skilled in the art of cookery, then turned ofttimes to still rougher duties.

Catherine had never fully recovered her health from the time she had been attacked by the fever, and her declining state of health had terminated in pulmonary consumption.

In the midst of much distress, and whilst Catherine lay sick unto death, Lilian's first child was born. New duties of every kind had devolved upon her, but in the hour of trial she was not found wanting.

Lilian was peculiar, perhaps, nevertheless it was a peculiarity which never spared self. She loved to use white toilet-covers, and white quilts, and snow-white draperies, as much as she had loved them in the home of her sunny youth; so that Catherine's sick-room always looked—at the cost of great trouble to herself,—clean, and the linen as white as if it had just come from the hands of the laundress. Another peculiarity doubtless, in one so poor especially, was her determination always to have a *white* baby, as she jestingly termed it; and when Catherine asked her what she meant by a white baby, she replied,—

"If I am so poor, Kate, that I must needs wash my baby's clothes myself, then I will do it; for no infant of mine shall be disfigured with colored frocks and socks,—a pure invention, I believe, to save a little work;" consequently this peculiar and eccentric Lilian not unfrequently was caught by Herbert ironing at midnight, after her own hands had washed the tiny frocks made of the soft embroidered muslin robes which she had herself worn in other and happier days.

The infant, Archey, whom she had named after her father, was thus never seen with other than a spotless frock of white muslin; and we can safely aver that neither colored socks nor petticoats disfigured the infant limbs of Lilian's child.

We are no admirer of Mistress Fanny Fern, nor was Lilian. The former lady sagely writes that she does not like houses in which chiffonniers and tables are not marked with the impress of baby fingers, and in which the state of the apartments does not bear indubitable marks of the presence of children.

Surely Fanny Fern has not the organ of neatness and good order well developed; if she had, she would abhor disorder and untidiness, however fond she may be of the baby portion of humanity. It is surely not hard to be fond of children and of good order at the same time. As to Lilian,—the refined and industrious Lilian,—she would, with many of our lady-readers, have been ready to swoon at the thought of an ill-kept household, dirty children, and an ill-managed table, around which little men and women are sometimes suffered noisily to clamor forth their wants.

But the little home was to undergo a change. Lilian tried very hard to wear her usually sunny smile, but sometimes the effort was in vain.

Catherine was dying. She could deceive herself no longer as to that. The orders at the studio in Newman Street were but few and far between, and Herbert had in vain tried to get a series of articles on the fine arts, on which he had devoted much of his leisure, into the pages of *Blackwood*.

He had met with just sufficient success as a writer to sharpen his appetite for more; he had yet to find out the difficulty of the task, unless backed by interest or influence.

There were moments in which he had been almost sorry that he had ever, under the delusive hope of doing better, induced the beautiful Lilian to link her fate with his. Such a thought, however, had never crossed the mind of the woman who was to be "made perfect in adversity."

The winter had passed away gloomily enough, and spring was clothing all things in her garniture of green; but Catherine Leslie faded slowly away. So gently did the summons come at last, that she herself, who had been ever on the watch, dreamed not that the moment was at hand. Lilian was alone in the house, and Catherine's long thin fingers had been some time nimbly at work embroidering a frock for the child. Suddenly it fell from her hands, and a deep sigh escaped her.

Lilian's quick ear detected the sound. The next moment she was at Catherine's side, her head resting on her shoulder. The soft rays of the April sun stole gently through the Venetian blind, which but a few moments before Catherine's own hand had drawn, complaining that the too strong light distressed her.

"Catherine, darling, look up!" exclaimed Lilian. "Speak to me. What is the matter?" she exclaimed, still unconscious that with that last sigh the golden fillet had burst its bonds, and that the immortal spirit had winged its flight to its eternal home. She then hurried from the house in quest of her own medical attendant, who returned with her to her desolate home. But who could now mistake? Not even Lilian, who beheld death for the first time. Oh, no! there it undoubtedly was. The pale, rigid countenance, the parted lips, the glazed eye told Lilian that Catherine Leslie was now an inhabitant of another world.

With reverent care, and bedewing the face of the

dead with her tears, Lilian placed those poor remains upon the couch; and after having closed, with trembling hands, the eyes which had so often beamed with love at her approach, she despatched the girl she had in her service to her husband; and, after having rocked her child to sleep, busied herself in those many melancholy duties which fall upon the inmate of a house in which death holds sway.

Poor Catherine! no master-mind was hers—of the bright intellect of her brother she had not a spark; yet all who knew admired and loved her, she possessed that wonderful tact of making others happy—of saying and doing things at the right time and in the right way; and the presiding genius of the little household seemed gone when good Catherine Leslie was called to the land of spirits. Lilian felt her loss daily, nay, hourly, for such persons as Catherine leave a void not easily filled up.

Poor Catherine! no more shall thy busy fingers arrange and dispose, and keep in order the little *et ceteras* about the house; never more shall thy voice be heard in reproof to the indolent, neglectful helps—for we may not call them servants—which thy narrow means alone allowed thee to keep.

Yet a good and gentle soul thou wert; and if not bright in intellect, thy soul was endowed with many virtues, which must surely earn thee a resting-place amongst the pure spirits above.

Thus thought Lilian as, a few days later, clad

in the deepest mourning, she stood beside a grave newly made, beneath which reposed the remains of Catherine Leslie. Over those same remains, however, when happier days dawned on her fortunes, she placed a simple but handsome monumental urn, on which was inscribed the one word—"Catherine." *Requiescat in pace.*

It told more to the passer-by of the wealth of love bestowed by the survivor on her who slept beneath, than the most high-sounding eulogium or flowery epitaph ever raised on monumental stone.

CHAPTER XI.

A THANKLESS OFFICE—A FEW WORDS ABOUT THE INSTITUTE OF NOTRE DAME AND ITS FOUNDRESS.

MARION is at length securely domiciled in Dublin; the sore parting with Lilian is healing up; and every day sees her duly, at the hour of nine, starting from the little cottage in which she has engaged apartments, at Sandy Mount, on her journey to her pupils in Rutland Square.

A pleasant family are these Burkes with whom Marion has had the good fortune to become acquainted; and, better than all, she soon became a favorite with the daughters, and through them with their parents.

Into the long future spread before her Marion often strove to penetrate, wondering what it would bring to her. She was happier, in a pecuniary point of view; contented, because she was striving to do her duty; cheerful generally, though often sorely worn by the querulous imbecility of her aged father.

The social frankness of the people charmed her; she found an utter difference between them and the English family with whom she had formerly discharged the duties of a governess.

Reserve is no doubt one of the characteristics of

John Bull, but forms no portion of those of our Milesian neighbors.

There is, however, a skeleton in every house; that in the family of Mr. Burke was large of its kind, for it had brought dissension into his household.

Rare elements for discord are doubtless at hand when the children of different parents share the same home; for Mr. Burke had unfortunately married a widow lady with a grown-up daughter; a silly idea no doubt, when his own eldest child was herself nineteen years old.

Now it so happened that Mrs. Burke was by no means an unkind, unamiable woman,—quite the reverse. It would be very hard to imagine that the owner of that fair, good-tempered face, always beaming with a kindly smile, was otherwise than a good, well-intentioned woman. Old enough, too, was she for the discharge of her duties as a stepmother, for Mr. Burke had not given pain to his daughters by putting over them a woman but little older than themselves, for the lady had passed her fortieth year; but, if the fact must be spoken, she was simply obnoxious because she stood in the place of the beloved mother whom these girls with their strong Irish affections and warm impulsive natures had idolised in life, and whose memory they reverenced in death. We take it to be a thankless office that assumed by the new Mrs. Burke; yet there were many things which should have operated in her favor, and insured for her a happier home, in so far, that by age she was well calculated to act in the place of a mother to those motherless girls. By nature she was far too kind to give pain to any human thing : nor was her union with Mr. Burke marked by any of those circumstances which often fatally militate against domestic happiness; she had a comfortable competency of her own bequeathed her by her deceased husband; her daughter was also provided for; and from her second marriage no young family had sprung to draw the affections of the father from the children of the first. How mischievous are these second marriages, when the children of the first have already past their girlhood. Mrs. Burke, worthy, good, amiable as she was, had made to herself an unhappy home. She had vainly tried to sound the depths of her step-daughters' hearts, to see if there was no unawakened cord which would respond to the affection she had been prepared to bestow upon them,—if the hearts of those girls, amiable, warm-hearted as they were, would always remain as a sealed book to her.

But the good lady was at length perforce obliged to abandon the task. Outwardly, she was treated with a cold civility, painful enough to the sensitive woman who yearned for affection which never perhaps might be hers. No, never; for the two girls, Kathleen and Ellen,—the one nineteen, the other seventeen years old,—considered her in the light of an intruder, and nothing else.

Her own daughter helped to aggravate the

unkindly feeling that prevailed; for Minna's impetuous temper rose at the injustice, as she deemed it, which was exercised by the daughters of her stepfather towards a mother whom she dearly loved.

Such was the aspect of things when the services of Marion were required for the two half-sisters as general instructress, and to teach painting to the elder daughter, who had passed some time at Canley.

A very few days was sufficient to let Marion into the secret. You see, these very unreserved girls would of course each enlighten her on the subject, and Marion speedily found herself occupying that most painful of all positions, the confidant of a divided family.

She guessed not, however, that her newly-made intimacy was to help much to heal the sore.

Kathleen had a secret of her own, which was soon communicated to Marion. She was resolved to marry and have a home of her own, in which no stepmother's influence would be brought to bear.

"And will not you marry, Miss Craig?" asked the young lady. "Oh how wretchedly dull your life must be with no companion but the poor old gentleman whom we saw when we called at Sandy Mount!"

"I am not dull, dear Miss Burke," replied Marion, with a laugh. "No one can be really dull whose time is occupied like my own."

"But you have not replied to both my questions; do you not intend to marry?"

"I shall never marry," was the reply, and the fair head drooped still lower over the sketch of her pupil, to which she was giving the last finishing touches. "But when it shall please God to call my father to Himself, I shall, if considered worthy, become a nun amongst the sisters of Notre Dame."

"But, dear Miss Craig, your father is not so *very* old. Suppose he were to live twenty years longer,—you know people *do* live till they are ninety and upwards,—what would you do then? you would be more than forty years old, wouldn't you? that would be rather old to go, would it not?" continued the catechist.

Something like a shudder passed through the frame of the devoted daughter as Kathleen rambled lightly on; it was but for one moment, as the thought flitted across her mind that her life might after all be always passed as now. She quickly recovered herself, however, and replied,—

"Yes, it would be rather old, Kathleen; and perhaps things might so turn out that, if I were obliged to live in the world for twenty long years, I might never go at all. But one must not look forward, for *'sufficient for the day is the evil thereof.'* There is nothing to be done but quietly to accomplish the work before us, and which for the time being, reason and religion alike show, *is* our work, and leave all the rest to our heavenly Father, for whilst we *propose*, God oftentimes *disposes*."

Whilst Marion had been speaking thus, her head still bent over the drawing, and a tear trembling in her eye, Minna and Ellen, the young ladies whose feuds were neither few nor far between, were gazing at her intently; and the former exclaimed,—

"One of these days, I think *I* should like to go into a convent; nay, Ellen, you need not quiz me so, I am quite in earnest, I assure you; and who knows, perhaps you may enter the same novitiate with me. But I was going to ask you, Miss Craig, to tell me something of the early foundation of the Order of Notre Dame; Kathleen, you know, was not many months at Canley, and I cannot get anything out of her."

"But our time is nearly up," said Marion, glancing at the timepiece; "what if you walk part of the way home with me when studies are over, and then I will gladly tell you the little that I know? Nay, I will ask Mrs. Burke to allow you all to spend the evening with me."

The invitation was gladly accepted; and, revived after their long walk by a refreshing cup of tea, Marion drew the girls around her, and commenced as follows:—

"I am going to tell you something about the Sisters of Notre Dame and their foundress, an account of which I read whilst in London.

"Julia Billiart, then, intimately known as Mother Julia, and foundress of the order, was born at Cuvilly, near Compiegne, and was a young woman of rare merit, ardent zeal, and solid and enlightened virtue. She was born in the year 1751, and was the daughter of parents but poorly favored by the gifts of fortune; but from a very early age God had drawn to Himself in a special manner this child of benediction.

"At the age of seven years she used to assemble around her the children of the parish to teach them the Catechism, which she was already able to explain with a wonderful intelligence.

"The cure of the parish failed not to notice the treasures hidden in this privileged one. He lavished on her every care. As she advanced in age, she advanced also in virtue; and God, who intended her to do great things for His glory, prepared her by willing that she should first pass through the crucible of tribulation. She became very ill; her malady withstood every remedy, and left her at the age of thirty years deprived of the use of both legs. She constantly suffered the greatest pain, and a violent contraction of the nerves of the jawbone took from her the possibility of speaking in an intelligible manner. The good cure, who had continued to direct her, brought her the holy communion daily; and Julia was fastened for twenty-two entire years to this bed of suffering, without the power of making a single step; and many ladies of position, brought by the venerable cure, came to seek from Julia examples of patience and resignation, and gave to her testimonies of their affectionate sympathy. But this tried soul was shortly to be deprived of these consolations, for the cure and the noble ladies were obliged to flee in order to escape the revolutionary persecution.

"No more sacraments; no more communions; no kind friends to comfort and console; and she now felt oppressed by the weight of her trials. But God, who suffers us not to be tempted above our strength, shortly restored her to peace and happiness. Julia's reputation for piety caused her to be suspected by the revolutionary party, and they endeavored to seize upon her person in order to subject her to shameful outrage; but she passed by in the midst of them, hidden in the bottom of a carriage, without being perceived.

"This was in 1794; and one of the ladies who had been intimate with Julia had taken refuge at Amiens, and she immediately wrote to her to persuade her to take up her abode in a small apartment in the Hotel Blin, in which she herself dwelt.

"Mademoiselle Marie Francoise, Vicomtesse Blin de Bourdon, whom God designed to labor with Julia for the salvation of souls, had also passed through a stormy life. She had come forth from the prison in which she had been detained with her family, they having been condemned to perish on the scaffold, but were restored to liberty at the moment of the fall of Robespierre; and she then resolved to renounce the world, and depriving herself of the advantages which her birth and fortune might have laid at her feet, she resolved to consecrate her whole life to prayer and good works.

"Julia had no sooner been brought to Mademoiselle Blin, than the latter made it a point of duty to take care of the suffering invalid whom Heaven had sent to her, and lavished upon her the attentions of a sick-nurse. In spite of the little attraction attending this charitable office, seeing that she did not even understand the language of the sick person, it established between the two one of those holy and strong friendships, the bonds of which death itself can only break.

"About the same time Julia received one of those consolations which her soul was always eagerly longing for. A virtuous priest also came to reside with the Vicomtesse Blin. He said mass in the invalid's chamber, gave her the holy communion daily, and presided at the religious exercises of many young persons who gathered themselves around Julia, giving to her the name of mother. The good priest was, however, sought after by the enemies of religion; and, in order to shelter himself from their domiciliary visits, he took refuge at Bethencourt, in a *chateau* belonging to two of the ladies who formed a portion of the society at the Hotel Blin. Thither mother Julia was removed, and Mademoiselle Blin de Bourdon resolved to follow her.

"They then undertook to teach young girls to read and write and knit, but still without thinking of consecrating themselves to the education of youth. The entire village soon became changed, and God crowned their first labors with success. But it was not till 1803 that they returned to Amiens. The Pere Varin, the Jesuit father from whose life I extract this little account, soon discovered the treasures of grace enclosed in this simple and generous soul; and, against all appearances, he believed her called to labor for the glory of God more than she had hitherto done. And when he communicated his thoughts to the humble invalid, she replied, '*My father, how is it possible that this can be done?*' She had recovered, however, for some time the use of speech; but her sufferings were still very intense.

"It was, however, at this time, I fancy, that she received in the house to which she had withdrawn with Mademoiselle Blin some zealous young ladies who wished to devote themselves to the instruction of poor young girls.

"In 1804, Pere Varin gave them a little rule by way of trial; and on the 2d of February the first members of this society devoted themselves, in the presence of the blessed sacrament, to the education of youth.

"About this time God granted to the lively faith of Mother Julia the cure of the paralysis under which she had so long suffered.

"In the October of the following year, the Vicomtesse and her friend, with two of their first associates, engaged themselves by vow to the work the thought of which God had inspired them with—this was the education of the middle class in towns and villages, still following merely the rule given them by the Pere Varin; and Julia then made overtures with Monsignor de Beaumont for the foundation of a house in Belgium. The prelate joyfully acceded, and she speedily prepared for the departure of this first colony.

"During her journey the foundress was called to Namur by the bishop of that place; and it was agreed that the following summer she should bring some sisters, in order to commence an establishment there.

"The foundation of Namur, of which Mademoiselle Blin was the first superioress, is the most important of all. From hence emerged, at a later date, those throngs of pious maidens who went forth to the deserts of America to give to the uncivilised female children, along with the bread to feed the body, the word of God to nourish the soul.

"As to Mother Julia, she was subjected to many painful trials—the bishop, and even Pere Varin himself, being prejudiced against her. In the end, after trials and contradictions which I cannot enter into, the Bishop of Amiens regretted the line of conduct he had pursued, and loudly declaring that he had been mistaken, acknowledged her for superioress-general of the order. The Sisters of Notre Dame were then established in various dioceses in France, and many foundations were established throughout Belgium.

"I have little more to tell you about Mother Julia, except that the excessive fear which the passage of foreign troops occasioned her in 1815, and the uneasiness she felt concerning some of her community who were in the very midst of the theatre of war, hastened her end : she died in the spring of the year 1816, her reputation being very great for virtue and prudence."

"And have you nothing to tell us of the Vicomtesse Blin, who had so narrowly escaped the guillotine?" inquired Ellen.

"Yes," replied Marion ; "she was chosen, by the unanimous voice of the sisterhood, to succeed her friend and spiritual mother ; and she governed with great virtue and prudence until her death, which happened in 1838. She was, we are told, a model of wisdom, meekness, and firmness combined ; and the order, under her government, made great progress. Since her death it has flourished more and more, bringing to every spot in which it has been established, the fruits of salvation which the Pere Varin had in view at the time of its foundation. It has extended not only through Belgium,—in which there are more than fifty establishments,—but also, as you are yourselves aware, to England and America ; counting in England ten houses, and almost as many in America. I must also add that in 1844 the Institute of Notre Dame was approved by the highest authority in the Church, which confirmed its constitutions and its rules."

"But, Miss Craig," said the curious Ellen, "I fancy I should like some more contemplative order; but just tell me a little about the rules, please."

"How ridiculous you make yourself, Ellen!" said her sister; "the idea of your thinking of being a nun! I am sure Miss Craig must be quite tired talking so much."

"Not I, Miss Burke," said Marion. "I am not soon tired of talking when I speak of the life led by my convent, friends so I will tell you, my dear Ellen, that the principal aim of the Sisters of Notre Dame is the instruction of the poor; so that in every house of the order there is an establishment for them—either a poor-school, an orphanage, or, as in Belgium, a reformatory and hospital for the aged and infirm. Sometimes there is not merely one, but, as is the case in London, Manchester, and Liverpool, as many as eight or nine poor-schools under their care, to which the Sisters go two by two every morning; whilst others have boarding-schools for the children of the middle or higher classes, according to the locality. Namur is, I am told, a name dear to every Sister of Notre Dame, as it is there each one takes her first steps in the religious life, receives the habit, and pronounces her vows. Do you not then see, Ellen, that the life of the Sister of Notre Dame partakes both of the active and the contemplative? they hear mass, and have an hour's meditation every morning, and"——

"An hour's meditation!" broke in Minna; "why, Miss Craig, that would never do for me. Why, I cannot give a quarter of an hour to anything of the sort, it is too hard for me."

"Nonsense, Minna," said Marion; "there is nothing hard at all in it. Do you find it hard to think? are you not thinking all day long? Why, then, should it be hard to reflect, only when we think of the happy eternity we all one day hope to enjoy? You see, however, there is more of the contemplative life than you appear to have bargained for. Do you think it would suit you?" Marion laughingly inquired; "there is rather more of the life of Mary than that of Martha in its practice, you see."

"Well," said Kathleen, "it is to be hoped they will both choose the same novitiate, Miss Craig, if they do take it into their heads to go into convents. I think Minna and Ellen should really go together, for their lives will be so peaceful, they will only know trial by name, unless they make a little by disputing together, as they are constantly doing now."

"My dear Miss Burke, I think you hold a very mistaken notion," said Marion. "As you have been a pensioner some few months at dear Canley, I should have thought you knew that the novitiate was not without its trials—some of them very rough ones for poor human nature."

"I am persuaded there are none of them which I could not patiently bear, and come off triumphantly," exclaimed Minna.

"Ah, my dear Minna," said Marion, "put in the saving clause, 'with God's help.' Who amongst us shall dare to say thus much of our daily trials, when striving to live as good Christians in the world, let alone the hourly aiming at that higher state of the most exalted virtue and perfection itself, required of those who follow the life of a religious? for remember, my dear Minna, self-denial in all its branches must be practised. In what, think you, the novitiate would present the greatest difficulties to you?"

"Really, I can scarcely tell you, Miss Craig, unless it be that I always like to have my own way," said Minna; "and I suppose I should not often get it there, added to which I am dearly fond of being what *you* call idle; and I suppose the nuns would fill my hands with work. I should not relish either the one or the other very much at first, I daresay; still there is a holy quiet about a convent life which pleases and interests me so much that I feel as if I could do battle with myself if I were allowed the chance."

"Dearest Minna," said Marion, taking the hand of her pupil within her own, "much more is wanting to you than this attraction to the life you speak of merely for its holy quietude and peace; yet the sweet call given but to a few may be still haply vouchsafed to you. I cannot promise you that in one iota you will be allowed to follow the bent of that indomitable will of yours which I have seen you so glad to follow; or that, save at stated hours of recreation, you will not be compelled to work,—to work, Minna, either with head or hands. The real essence of a religious life consists in obedience, or the perfect renunciation of your own will; and an idle nun would be indeed an anomaly in the cloister, in which each sister is expected to work according to her talent for the weal of the whole community; but bear in mind, Minna, that as, to use a familiar proverb, 'Rome was not built in a day,' so our faults and imperfections are not cured in an hour. It is as necessary to be patient with one's self in the practice of virtue as in any of the daily occurrences of life. All are not saints, you know, when they enter convents."

"No; I should think not, indeed," said Ellen. "Why, Minna, do you not remember Margaret and Emma Gisborne? I'm sure they were not paragons of perfection, nor did they set an over good example to any one else; they were passionate, self-willed girls. I am quite certain Minna and myself, though we have a quarrel sometimes, are perfect angels compared to them. Margaret came back before she had been two months in the Loretto Convent, to which she had begged hard to be sent; and Emma, well, Emma stayed, and became a professed nun amongst the Benedictine nuns in some English convent. So, I suppose, she cured herself of her bad habits."

"You need not suppose it, Ellen, but may take it for granted," said Marion. "I have no doubt, were you now in the company of the young lady you speak of, you would find her the very reverse of what she once was; for, depend upon it, her self-will and pride would be the failings on which the first onslaught would be made; they must, I will not say have eradicated them, perhaps, but at least they must have been subdued, or most assuredly she could never have been admitted to her religious profession. So if the young lady went full of faults to the good Benedictines, let us be quite certain that she has long ere this laid many of her failings at the foot of the cross, or you would have seen her back as well as her sister. Now I hope I have not frightened you," she added, "with my narration of what is required of a young person before she can be admitted to the religious state."

"Not I, dear Miss Craig," exclaimed Minna; "I only wish I were half as patient and meek and humble as I know you to be, then"——

"Hush, love, you must not talk in that way," said Marion, placing her finger on her lips. "Silly Minna! how do you know how much I may feel within me that I have to overcome?"

"Oh, nonsense, Miss Craig!" was the reply of Ellen. "You know we have heard how rich Mr. Craig was, and now look at the change! I think you a perfect saint to walk through the wet and cold and never say a word; and bear with matchless patience your poor papa's imbecility, for you always have a smile on your face; and I think *we* have tried your patience often enough, and yet"——

"Never so sorely as now, my dear girls," said the poor young governess, starting up, her face covered with blushes.

"Go on, go on, Ellen," said the mischievous Minna; "it is only her humility makes her speak in that way."

The gentle Marion turned away as if she had not heard the last playful sally of her gay young friends; she tied on her bonnet in the adjoining room, in order to accompany them on their homeward way; then placed a comfortable supper before the querulous old gentleman, who drew her face down to his, stroked tenderly the golden curls which fell on his withered forehead, calling her his best and dearest daughter, and prayed that Heaven's blessing might descend upon her head, and then exclaimed,—

"But where are you going, my love? You are not going to leave me for long, Marion? Will you be back in ten minutes?"

"I shall not be away a bit more than an hour, papa; and Mrs. Murphy will look to you, lest you should want anything before my return," said Marion.

"An hour! a *whole* hour! It is very long to be left alone, after you have been away from me the best part of the day," murmured the old gentleman, in the same querulous tone.

"I cannot help it; you *know* I cannot help it,"

she said, with a gesture of impatience, hurrying from the room as she spoke. Yet even as the words trembled on her lips, she reproached herself for her want of patient forbearance. Her heart knew its own secret better than the young girls whose company she had so recently quitted; better than the wives and mothers who pointed her out as a model for the young to copy; better than the whole world, save one, who for her guidance and direction held the secrets of her heart within his keeping in the tribunal of penance. Marion, the Marion who had but just now spoken so prettily and so well of the duty of subduing passion, knew too well the master-passion, the predominant failing of her soul, to take to herself the praise which young and old alike bestowed upon her. Poor Marion, like most of us, you can preach well to others; and, like many well-meaning persons, you sadly want patience with yourself. You have not yet learnt the practice of that virtue on which you have descanted to your pupils this very evening; you feel that inward commotion within you, that interior disturbance, where you would fain that all were at peace. And for a moment you yield, and in a voice and gesture and manner you betray the emotion of your heart; and *then*, instead of repairing the evil, you become impatient with yourself. Small wonder, but twenty-one summers have passed over thy fair young head; why, you have yet to learn that the strife may go on for thirty, forty, fifty years,—nay, for a whole life, and still——

Ay, reader, do you not know, as well as we ourselves, that ever, ever we may strive, and yet that the night in which no man can work *may* come, *does* come, and still the master-passion remains unsubdued?

Child of earth, lose not courage; *he*, that poor, querulous, imbecile man, is left thee, perhaps, in mercy, so that by patient, meek endurance thou mayst merit a bright hereafter. Well for us, indeed, if in such a spirit we can accept our trials. Fleeting as an April shower, its pearly drops caught up by the sun's warm rays, were the tears which had lingered, just *one* moment, in Marion's eyes, and dashing them hastily aside, with a bright smile again on her face, she re-entered the room in which she had left her pupils, and walked some way home with them, till she resigned them into the hands of the housekeeper, who had come to meet them; and then returned to her certainly far-from-cheerful home, for an hour's reading before she retired to rest. Shall we own the truth? this was Marion's pleasantest hour,—her hour of recreation, of amusement. Well, it was so to her, you see; for the earlier hours of the day were engaged in teaching, then some two or three in the company of one who had long lost all claim to the title of companion; who rarely spoke, or if he did, it was to moan out some querulous complaint, or utter some remark which told of utter absence of intellect, of perfect imbecility. Surely this could not be called relief, after the anxious duties of the day.

CHAPTER XII.

UNDER A CLOUD—TRICKS OF THE TRADE.

"It is an old saying, that the darkest hour comes before the dawn. Herbert, I do not think we can well have a darker than this," said Lilian, as, with eyes streaming with tears, she sat one burning August morning making up a black dress, as a mourning garb for her firstborn, its pale, cold little form now lying stretched in its gray coffin, in the adjoining room.

"Alas, my Lilian!" replied her husband, replacing in its envelope a letter he had just read, "it *has* been a comfort amidst our own misery to know that poor Marion and your father were going on pretty quietly; but even *that* has come to an end. I really do not like, or feel satisfied with myself, even in our cruel emergency, using the five-pound note that darling girl has sent us this morning; and yet, without doing so, how are we possibly to lay our poor child in its grave? But try and eat, Lilian; your strength will quite go, if you do not take some support; and yet there is nothing to tempt the sickly palate here," he added, as he pushed aside the weak tea and simple bread and butter, which yet stood untasted before her.

"I cannot eat, Herbert," she exclaimed, dropping the work on which she had been engaged, for she could scarcely see through her fast-falling tears. "It is as you say, so hard to take poor Marion's hard-earned money, and see no way of repaying her; for, mark my words, my husband, as soon will yonder sun fall from the heavens as you will have justice done you by the disappointed author-publisher, for whom your brain has worked so many weary hours. Talk to me of picture-dealers; yes, *they* are bad enough, no doubt, but yet not so bad as this man Manton."

At this moment a double knock was heard at the door; and then Lilian heard herself called by name.

"How vulgar!" she excaimed, as she left the room. "I fear it will be some time before I shall get accustomed to all the horrors of our present situation."

Herbert sighed heavily. If Lilian *was* fastidious, what then? Contrast her former stately home with the little square in Lambeth in which they rented an unfurnished first floor; for they had quitted some three months since the pretty, though humble, cottage in Brixton. A back street has many nuisances, Lilian was wont to say. The eternal cries of water-cresses and Yarmouth herrings in the morning—the herd of unkempt, noisy children, who constantly hung about the doors of the houses, congregating in knots of fifteens and twenties, as they left a ragged school hard by—the

Babel of discordant sounds in the afternoon—the repetition of the morning nuisance, with the increase of the vendors of sundry viands for the four o'clock tea or early supper of the mechanics, of whom not a few reside in the small squares and back streets of Lambeth,—all made up a medley of horrors on a small scale for the intellectual, gifted Lilian: we should not say on a small scale, however, for to the quietly or studiously inclined, as well as to the delicate in health, whose throbbing heads so pant after quiet, what is so terrible as a noisy neighborhood? However, the back streets, which in a poor locality are *always* unquiet, must of necessity be the dwelling-places of the needy lady and gentleman; and Heaven help them in their habitations, poor souls, especially if they have weak nerves! The Sundays, too; why, really Lilian almost wished sometimes that men whose views were as strait-laced and narrow as a certain nobleman we wot of, could gain their sanctimonious, rigid ends regarding the Sabbath; far better, she would say, than this eternal din. *Cats-meat!* ay, even the euphonious cry of cats-meat on the Sunday morning, when sundry hands were lifted up through area railings, and stretched-out arms through half-open doors, betraying that the mistress of the house was still *en deshabille*, having enjoyed a prolonged rest *because* it was Sunday; and then the afternoons, when cry succeeded cry, strawberries and other fruits of the season, followed by 'winkles —we presume the word is abbreviated for the sake of the breath of the crier; however, these low sights and sounds formed a category of horrors for the sensitive, nervous lady, whose hard fate compelled her to endure them. To return from our digression.

The visitor was a widow lady, a Mrs. Cecil, a good woman and a very zealous Catholic, who had been the friend of Catherine long before Lilian's marriage with her brother.

Her means were small; we may safely add that, had they corresponded with the wishes of her heart, the Leslies would not have been suffered to know distress.

Lilian's letter of the previous day had told her of the death of her child, and the good lady had come to pay her a visit of condolence.

The loss of her child, at the age when childhood is most engaging, had been a severe blow to Lilian; and the energy, the fortitude she had shown through all her severe trials, seemed on the point of forsaking her at this troubled crisis of her life.

Herbert heard the door of the adjoining room softly opened, and then the deep sobs of his wife. She yielded sadly to her grief. He felt cruelly apprehensive lest, if this should continue, her own health would sink under her heavy grief.

At length she returned with her friend to the room in which she had left her husband; and a spark of the haughty Lilian of former days still lurked under the subdued demeanor into which she had been schooled by misfortune, by the look of contempt she threw around the room, and the tone of voice, betokening wounded pride, in which she said, as her eye fell on the scantily-spread table,—

"Really, Mrs. Cecil, unless I knew you well, and esteemed you much, you would never have been welcomed into this humble domicile of ours. I tell Herbert I can bear to see no one till some little gleam of better fortune shall attend our efforts."

"My dear Lilian," said the visitor, "pray do not be so cast down, the darkest hour often precedes the dawn; depend on it there will yet be a silver lining to the cloud, and that Herbert's genius, both as an artist and an author, will ultimately meet with its reward."

"I doubt it very much," replied Lilian; "that is to say, if he is to depend on the *joint-profit* system, of which the constant result appears to be that there is nothing for the wretched author to receive. Mrs. Cecil," she added, her fine eyes filling with tears, "I cannot tell you how much we have had to undergo, and that at the very time my poor baby was dying, because, whilst we see the title placarded on the walls, and are reading very favorable reviews, and behold it in the windows of the circulating libraries, Mr. Manton yet tells Herbert that his book has not paid its expenses. Ah, you know not what we suffered," she continued, "before we gave up our house; threatened with an execution for poor-rates, and then obliged to sacrifice part of our furniture in order to pay up our rent."

"But, my dear Lilian," said Herbert, "the rates must be paid, you know, and the poor must be cared for."

"Yes, by the cold charity of the union," she replied. "Oh for the days when England was Catholic, when the good religious succored the needy and starving poor, instead of persons, struggling with poverty like ourselves, having the last farthing wrung from them in the form of poor-rates! Look you, Mrs. Cecil," she continued, "in this very house there lives a poor young dressmaker; the father is out of employment, and the three children are all too young for work. A week since Elizabeth had an order to make up some mourning; it was required in a few days; and for three nights that poor girl and her mother were hard at work, or else they could not have finished it in time. This morning she received twenty-five shillings in payment; and she came to me, with her eyes red and inflamed from close application to the black work, to tell me that it must all go to pay the quarter's poor-rate. Is it not shocking to think of the way in which the genteel poor are mulcted for the destitute who have to seek the refuge of the poor-house?"

"Ah, indeed! and a sore refuge, too, it is," replied Herbert. "We may truly say that England has lost by her Reformation, or deformation, for she has sent her poor to the walls of a workhouse; they were the dearly-loved children of a Church which taught them that poverty had a sacredness in its character, because it gave them a closer resemblance to Him who honored poverty by bearing it in His own person, whilst now it is treated as if it were a crime and the very pariah of society. The convict within the walls of his prison is better fed and cared for than the innocent and suffering poor. What, then, has England gained? except it be for those struggling with misfortune themselves, an often overwhelming rate, whilst the whole land is studded with poorhouses."

"Herbert grows eloquent, Mrs. Cecil," said Lilian, smiling. "As to myself, I must tell you I look back with a bitter self-reproach on the past. I remember old times, and the extravagance and luxury in which we lived; and when my ears are dinned with the discordant sounds by which they are constantly assailed in this little square, and Herbert pauses, and protests he can write no more till the place is quieter, then I remember, and wish that it were mine again to enjoy the quietude of the country, which I once so disliked."

"That, I am well assured, will one day again be yours," said Mrs. Cecil, rising and bidding adieu to Herbert, Lilian accompanying her to the street door. Then after good-bye had been said, and there was no longer time for expostulation, the kind friend, as she shook Lilian warmly by the hand, pressed therein a five-pound note, whispering,—

"Take it, love, for the expenses of dear baby's funeral."

The young author was indeed bitterly smarting under the effects of the delusion attendant on the joint-profit system; and the dark cloud had gradually been growing darker and darker, just as you have watched it settle over your own fortunes, reader, if it has ever been your fate to be tried in the rough school of adversity, if so, you well know what a sad thing it is to wake in the dead hour of the night, and the moment you open your eyes, whilst you are still writhing under some unexpected blow, to have the thought of your great trouble rush upon you; to toss and turn upon your bed, feverish and restless, not knowing how to meet the coming morrow, or face the difficulties the dawn is sure to bring with it. Ah, it is a very terrible thing, this looking from day to day, and yet how many are thus doomed in this great metropolis, especially amongst the geenteel poor, so to run out the measure of their days! And is it not true that the trouble in the sleepless, wakeful hours of night is far more terrible than the same trouble in the day? so both Lilian and Herbert felt it; and then to complete it all, came the death of the child, and the news that, in consequence of a change of circumstances in the family of Mr. Burke, Marion's services would not be required beyond the next quarter; so that their poor hearts were almost crushed under their sudden access of trouble.

Lilian, however, bore up bravely, like a true-hearted woman, as she was; only, you know, like all of us, there were moments when the trouble seemed too heavy to bear, and then she would give vent to a hearty flood of tears; perhaps they would be tears in which impatience as well as grief bore some part; if so, she soon took herself to task, and resolved to renew her confidence in that Providence which never tempteth us beyond our strength.

Trouble, especially pecuniary trouble, is very hard to bear; we all shrink from its approach; but I have often thought that it must surely be more grievous when, as was the case with Lilian, it visits those who for several years have been the favored children of fortune, and then are suddenly plunged into severe distress.

CHAPTER XIII.

FROM SUNSET TILL SUNRISE; OR, MAID, BRIDE, AND WIDOW.

FOUR months have passed since the pleasant evening on which our friend Marion held the conversation with her pupils anent the Order of Notre Dame, and in that time many changes have taken place; Minna has left home in order to begin her novitiate at Namur, thus proving the truth, that many a word said in jest turns out to be earnest in the end. One source of discord, then, was removed from the household; but all is not honey yet, "making it apparent," says Mrs. Burke, "that it was not my poor Minna who was always in fault; very far from it, indeed, for the two sisters are often at variance with each other, and not over well behaved to me."

Kathleen, however, was shortly to quit the parental roof, to become a wife, and mistress of a household; and the thought of the new importance she was about to acquire made her exceedingly happy. The wedding *trousseau* was purchased, the day had long been fixed upon, the marriage was considered an eligible one, and all things seemed as prosperous as could be desired. The evening of the day previous to the wedding had arrived, and the flutter of excitement and anxiety in which Kathleen had been during the whole day was at its height, as the time approached for the return of Leonard Moran from an expedition some twenty miles from Dublin, which he had made that day, solely with the view of procuring a wedding present which he had commissioned a relation, who had just returned from London, to procure for his bride.

It was a very valuable gift, being nothing less than a diamond bracelet; and, unwilling to hazard the custody of anything so expensive to strange hands, the young man had left home in the morning with the promise that he should bring *his* wedding gift to Kathleen that evening, and should not fail to arrive by the train at 7 P.M. Marion could on no account be spared; she had been invited to be one of the wedding party on the following day, and it was only with some little difficulty that she could get away for the night.

She was to accompany Kathleen and her sister to the railway station to meet Leonard Moran, leaving Mrs. Burke very busy, and all smiles and good humor. And if some of these smiles, Mrs. Burke, are because it will be the last night Kathleen will pass beneath her father's roof, we can still almost forgive you. In high spirits, the two young ladies, accompanied by Marion, tripped off to the station. They were, however, a little before the time; but they amused themselves in walking up and down the platform, talking very gaily, little thinking of the dark cloud that was gathering around them.

At last Kathleen noticed that the hour was past, and made inquiry of the guard. She was told that the train had been due at seven, but would doubtless arrive shortly.

"How very tiresome!" she exclaimed. "I feel so impatient till I see Leonard; but let us step into the waiting-room," she added, "for see, there is a knot of people collecting at the other end of the platform, and it is so unpleasant to get into a crowd."

Thus speaking, she turned into the waiting-room, and another ten minutes passed away; but Marion was abstracted and uneasy, for her quick ear, as she left the platform, had caught the words, "Railway accident." A painful thought occurred to her as she looked at the blooming happy girl before her. What if there *had* been an accident, and harm had befallen Leonard Moran?

At length Kathleen became anxious, and again returned to the platform. The knot of persons who had previously assembled had doubled, nay, trebled, their numbers, and a train was heard speedily advancing. This, then, was the train which contained Leonard; and breaking from Marion's arm, which she hastily dashed aside, she pushed through the crowd, followed by her friend and her sister. Marion had heard the words, "Telegraphic message." There *had* been an accident, then; the message had been received whilst they were idling away the time in the waiting-room. On, on through a now excited throng, Kathleen forced her way; the words, so alarming in their import had reached her ear. Had Leonard escaped? Was *he* the occupant of one of those carriages which slowly, oh, so slowly for her excited mind, steamed their way into the station? Once, only once, she turned.

"Ellen—Miss Craig," she murmured, with a rigid face and ashen lips, "they say there has been an accident to the train running from Kildare —watch every gentleman leaving those carriages. O God, support me, should he not be there!"

"Thirteen killed and wounded!" exclaimed a second-class passenger as he leaped on to the platform; "there has been a frightful scene, and the line blocked up for nearly an hour."

His words fell like ice on the heart of Kathleen. She had watched the last man descend; Leonard Moran was *not* amongst the passengers.

"Come home, dear Miss Burke," said Marion; "doubtless your father will at once go and see himself the cause of Mr. Moran's absence."

"Home!" exclaimed Kathleen, in an accent expressive of astonishment; then she feebly tottered to a guard who stood a few paces distant, and inquired when the next train left for Kildare.

"In ten minutes, miss," replied the man; "you can get your ticket at once, the booking-office is open."

"Miss Craig," said Kathleen, turning to Marion,

"tell my father that I could not return home in this suspense—every hour is an age ; till I see how it has fared with Leonard, go you home with Ellen."

"I shall not leave you, Kathleen," said Marion. "I will put Ellen into a cab, and accompany *you*, if you are resolved on going."

Expostulation was useless, Kathleen *had* resolved already, and seeing the terrified Ellen safely from the station, Marion gave her a message to her father, to say that, in the excited state in which Kathleen was at present, she would not suffer her to put into execution by herself the rash determination she had made. A few moments more and the huge engine came puffing into the station. The friends took their places in a first-class carriage, and Marion felt almost frightened as she gazed on the stony countenance of the girl, which one short hour before had been radiant with joy and happiness.

Kathleen spoke not a word during their journey ; but Marion noticed that the small hands were clenched convulsively together, and then placed on her heart. As they advanced nearer to the spot which they knew to have been the scene of the collision which had deprived some of life, and had horribly mutilated others,—for here and there beyond the line, lying in an adjacent field, they beheld the wrecks of carriages, their shattered *debris* showing how terrible the disaster had been, —a sickening feeling came over Marion, and she narrowly escaped fainting ; but a glance at the pale, sorrowful face of the unhappy Kathleen told her that she should not be the one whose energies should fail at the very moment in which she might be of use.

Slowly the train wended its way into the station ; and as soon as it came to a stand-still, a crowd of anxious persons sprung from the carriages, eager to know whether their missing relatives were amongst the dead or wounded.

"The bodies of those who have been killed by the collision, miss, are placed in a room at the station, in order to await the coroner's inquest, which will be held to-morrow morning," said a guard, in answer to the question put by Marion.

"Have the goodness to show the way," she said ; "we are anxious to see if a gentleman who was to have returned by the last train is amongst the"——

She could not finish the sentence ; but, with Kathleen leaning heavily on her arm, she followed the steps of the guard.

They entered the room now dimly lighted by the setting sun ; it shed a sickly, ghastly glare on the upturned and dead faces of the unfortunate sufferers from one of those disastrous collisions so frequently attendant on railway travelling.

"One, two, three, four," counted Marion, as, with that almost inanimate form leaning on her arm for support, and dragging rather than walking beside the long tables on which the bodies of the dead had been placed, she glanced successively at the countenances of each; some, where internal injuries had been the cause of immediate death, looking as placid as though they were asleep; others, and these were not a few, for they numbered eight in all, were shockingly mutilated, so that they could scarcely be recognized save by their clothes.

"He is not here, God be thanked!" were the first words spoken by Kathleen, as they paused beside the corpse of an aged man, whose white locks were crimsoned with his blood. "Take me away; oh, take me to *him!*" she added, still dragging heavily on the now aching arm of Marion, who herself, sick and faint at the ghastly sight before her, found that she must summon all her resolution, or that she should speedily lose the power of looking after herself, much less one so utterly dependent on others as the poor girl who clung so helplessly to her side.

Turning to the guard, then, she begged him to direct her to the inn to which the sufferers yet surviving had been removed. It was a simple village inn, not three hundred yards from the railway station, to which they bent their steps. The place was thronged by persons of various descriptions; some lurking about from motives of mere curiosity, others in torture, till they could ascertain the probable fate of those whom they had come to seek.

The man, however, speedily made room for the two ladies to pass, the unutterable anguish depicted on the deathly countenance of Kathleen telling him that hers was one of the cases which would not brook delay.

Marion immediately asked to speak to the mistress of the house, and found that there were at that moment three cases which required surgical aid, and that all were more or less dangerous.

She was yet conferring with the woman as to how they could best obtain admittance, so as to ascertain if either of these three sufferers should be the unfortunate Leonard, when a gentleman, habited in a sober suit of black, and whom the landlady addressed as Dr. Gannon, entered the room. Marion instantly addressed him:—

"You can, perhaps, give us some information, sir. One of the sufferers in this house is probably the gentleman we seek. Papers may be on his person, for he had articles of value with him at the time of this terrible disaster. Leonard Moran is the name of the friend of whom we are in search."

Dr. Gannon cast a sympathising look on the trembling form and pale face of Kathleen, and then took his tablets from his pocket, reading aloud— "Sufferer from concussion of the brain; name and address not known. Patrick Delany; both legs broken. Leonard Moran; severe internal injury."

"I have this moment left the gentleman," said the doctor, with so grave an aspect that Marion knew that Kathleen's fate was sealed.

Kathleen grasped the doctor by the arm, exclaiming, "Show me the way to Mr. Moran's room; I must see him without a moment's delay."

"Is this young lady his wife?" said the doctor. "The slightest excitement will be fatal. I warn you of this beforehand."

"No; but twelve short hours would have given me that title," said Kathleen, in so despairing a tone that the eyes of the doctor were humid with tears.

"I scarcely like introducing you to him in the precarious state in which he lies," he said. "Will you, however, promise me to control your feelings?"

"I will," she replied, shivering as though in an ague fit, and following the doctor, as he led the way to the small, ill-furnished room in which Leonard lay.

No power on earth, however, would have made Dr. Gannon commit what he knew professionally was an imprudent action; but then his patient had, he was aware, ordered a telegraphic message to be sent immediately to Rutland Square. The excitement attendant on meeting his friends must come in a very short space of time—why not at once?

Kathleen tottered, still leaning on Marion, into the darkened room. She stood beside the bed on which he was stretched; she leaned over him; and her rigid countenance, pale as marble, unrelieved by a single tear, told him how much she suffered.

"I cannot live many hours, Kathleen," he feebly whispered. "Is there any request you wish to make, my own darling?—if so, speak whilst I have yet power to reply."

"Yes, my Leonard," said Kathleen, as she sank on her knees beside the bed. "To-morrow would have united us at the foot of the altar," she added, placing her hand in his; "let us now"——

"Be made one," he feebly replied, catching the meaning of her words.

At that moment the door opened, and Kathleen's father entered the room, accompanied by his wife.

Leonard Moran gave them a look of recognition, and exclaimed, "Let us be made one—it is Kathleen's wish."

At the same moment he signed to Dr. Gannon: the latter placed in the hands of Kathleen a small parcel, telling her that the gentleman had directed him to give it to her in case of his death before she arrived. She knew well that its contents—a token of love for her—had been purchased at the cost of his own life, as but for that tiny parcel Leonard would not have left Dublin on the day in question. Her tears fell thick and fast on the glittering baubles which the casket contained. In the parcel, disclosed to view, there lay the diamond bracelet, and folded in a heap of cotton and wool the tiny gold ring, which she was to wear on her finger the following day.

The change in the countenance of Leonard sufficiently announced to his afflicted friends that his time on earth,—nay, his very hours were numbered; but amidst the breathless silence of all, broken only by the deep sobs of Kathleen; he whispered out the words,—

"Dr. Gannon, do not deceive me; how long have I yet to live?"

"Not many hours," was the reply; "mortification will speedily set in."

"Send for a priest," he said, and covering his face with his hands, he lay for some moments engaged in deep and earnest prayer.

Leonard Moran was a devout Catholic, and as the nuptials of the Morans were to have been in strict accordance with good old Catholic usages, both bride and bridegroom had prepared themselves by approaching the tribunal of penance.

In less than half an hour the priest arrived; a venerable man; the parish priest of a simple country congregation. He had been told a gentleman was dying, one of the sufferers from the recent collision; but he was not aware that he had to confer the sacrament of matrimony also, till Mr. Burke, having drawn him aside, briefly explained the case.

What a contrast did the wedding party, assembled in that small, mean, scantily-furnished room, present to that which had been projected for the morrow!

Oh, death, indeed, to every worldly hope for the poor, pale, half-fainting bride, who, raising her head from the friendly bosom of poor Mrs. Burke, now stood beside the bed, repeating the words of the marriage-service, her hand clasped in one scarce colder than her own. And the solemn rite concluded, the priest prepared to administer that other holy sacrament—the mystery of ineffable love, the Eucharist—to the dying man. Ah! on the morrow the husband and his bride—the latter now to return to a widowed home—were to have sealed their compact *together* in that holy sacrament. And then intimating that before the night grew late he would call again to administer the rite of extreme unction, he returned home.

Not for a moment did the heart-broken Kathleen leave the pillow of the ill-fated Leonard, and a gush of bitter tears burst forth as he informed her that he had already named her in the will which he had drawn up some time since; then banishing earthly matters from his mind, he bid her repeat the psalms and the litany for the dying, in which she was still employed when the priest re-entered the room.

It was a sudden revulsion this which hurried from the world one in whose veins the tide of life had flowed so freshly but a few hours since, and who had promised to himself such a morrow.

"*Such* a morrow ours was to have been!" he faintly gasped forth, still holding the hand of his bride; "but the sun has gone down for me whilst it is yet day. God's will be done."

"Amen," replied the priest; "it will rise for you in a never-ending eternity."

Leonard lingered through the night; that night of horror to all who kept watch by his death-bed, for they could not avoid contrasting it with their anticipated happiness. Marion had sent a telegraphic message to her landlady, begging her to try and make her father understand what had happened, and endeavor to reconcile him to her absence for this one night. Just as the first crow of the cock was heard, and the first streak of light was visible in the east, there was a perceptible change in the sufferer; the breath came shorter and shorter; and as the golden rays of the rising sun broke into the death-chamber, they served only to show more vividly the gray shadow of death which was passing over the pale, quiet face.

"All nature seems springing into life and light," thought Marion, "whilst the being destined to immortality bursts the bonds which confines it to its mortal tabernacle."

Suddenly a deep sob burst from the lips of Kathleen; her ear, keen to every sound, as her heart was more alive to every instinct of affection where Leonard was concerned, had caught a low sigh, heard by no ear save her own; her hand, clasped hitherto with all the tenacity of love, felt the grasp relax; her watchful eye beheld the shadow deepen, and knew that it was death; she could bear no more, nature must have its vent, and, with a low, bitter, wailing cry, the widowed bride sank senseless into her father's arms.

CHAPTER XIV.

BEHIND THE CURTAIN.

The sod upon the little grave in the cemetery at Norwood was already green with the verdure of another spring; but Lilian's heart had not ceased to ache over the loss of her firstborn, added to which trial still pressed heavily on the whole family. There were moments when she felt acutely, too, the burden of her father being thrown entirely on her younger sister through her own marriage, though at the time it took place she had had reason to hope that a prosperous change would work such a revolution in Leslie's affairs, that they should be able to offer a home themselves to the now infirm Mr. Craig. Thus Lilian felt a species of amiable envy, if we may so speak, towards Marion, who she knew had, at the stern call of filial duty, remained in the world for an indefinite period, struggling on till a change in their own circumstances, or the ultimate death of her father, should set her free; whilst she had, by uniting herself to Herbert, left her sister all the merit of her sacrifice; and she daily became more uneasy on Marion's account, having heard from her of the changes taking place in Mr. Burke's family, and her proposed return home—"to do what?" To take a cottage at Torquay, or some such place; let apartments, and give private lessons. "For," said Marion in her note, "the state of my health more and more unfits me for the hard life of a daily governess."

She was one day sitting musing thus, when she saw Herbert cross the square in the company of a gentleman, a stranger to herself. She knew he had left home to work all day at his studio in one of the back streets in Soho—that in Newman Street had been long since given up—and opened the door, wondering what had brought him back. She then ascertained that he had met this gentleman, whom he introduced by the name of Mr. Richmond, and whose portrait he had formerly taken, at a short distance from home, and having fallen into conversation, the two had returned together to Herbert's lodgings.

The simple mourning worn by Lilian could not disguise her extreme beauty, whilst her conversation betrayed that she was also an intellectual and accomplished woman.

"Will there be a silver lining to the cloud?" she thought, as the stranger exhibited a lively interest in their affairs, prefacing his remarks with,—

"You should be living in a superior place to this, Leslie, had you your deserts. Let me have your papers upon the fine arts. If *Blackwood* has rejected them, some one else may like them; try all the trade round, rather than be repulsed and downcast at one rejection. I am myself somewhat of a literary man, you know, and perhaps may be able to give you a little help, as well as recommend persons to come to your studio. However, take for your motto these two words, *Nil desperandum*, and rest assured that in the end you will come off triumphant."

"I assure you Herbert is very much discouraged," said Lilian. "I do not know which he has found the worst, literature or painting; we are not in the clique, Mr. Richmond, either amongst artists or authors, and may go on starving, I fear, till doomsday, unless he can push himself forward."

"Quite right, my dear madam; your husband is *not* one of a clique, as you rightly say; he is what is facetiously termed by the literary fraternity an *out-sider;* but we must see if he cannot push himself forward as others have done. You have never 'written to order,' I presume?" he said, turning to Herbert.

"Written to order!" replied the latter; "I do not even know what is meant by the term."

"Admirable simplicity!" said Mr. Richmond, with a laugh. "Why, 'writing to order' means having a plot given to you, and then filling it up yourself; writing a tale, in fact, to a certain given plot."

"I could not write in fetters, Mr. Richmond," rejoined Leslie; "my imagination must be left to wander as it will, fancy free. I could write a far better imaginative work, and I am sure I may say so without conceit, than nine-tenths of those with which the literature of the present day is polluted; but no filling up another person's plot for me. I could not work if bound to follow the rule laid down by another."

"Perfectly right, Leslie, follow your own," said his visitor; "only, to work at once, and with energy; and, mark my words, you will at last come off triumphant. As to the studio, you will see a friend of mine to-morrow who will employ you on an historical painting. And now *au revoir*, Mrs. Leslie," he said, rising and shaking hands with Lilian, and then accompanied her husband on his way to Soho.

Then Lilian sat down to paint, for she earned a little money sometimes that way; but her brush would keep dropping from her hand, and she fell into a regular musing fit,—such as you fall into yourself very often when you hope for some change in your fortunes,—and she weaved out in her sunny imagination a bright prospect for the future, which she beheld in perspective. A pleasant little home, with an aged white-haired man sitting by *her* fireside; and then that dear Marion could go to Canley as soon as she wished, though we are fain to say that this wicked Lilian sighed very deeply at the thought, and even dropped a tear in grief at the reflection that Marion would *not* be happy except in one particular way, that way involving an utter separation from all the world.

Let us leave her with this glimmer of better fortune,—for there *is* a break in the cloud,—and go to the sister isle, and see what Marion is doing.

CHAPTER XV.

THE SHADOW ON THE HEARTH.

THE shadow is on the hearth still—a shadow never to be removed is on the sweet face of Kathleen, the widowed bride; it follows her everywhere—when she visits the stately monument at Glasnevin—when she sits in her own old room at Rutland Square; in the busy streets by day—in the quiet, silent hours of the night—in the very sanctuary itself, this shade of an unsubdued, never-to-be-forgotten sorrow pursues her still. *"For me, for me,"* is ever her despairing cry,—*"for me he met his death!"*

Deep and strong is the passion of love in the heart of this impulsive Irish girl. I wonder will it ever awaken to any other tune. Those who knew Kathleen never imagined that her heart was capable of such a depth of affection; they had thought of her, spoken of her, as of an amiable, but somewhat frivolous girl; all who knew her were surprised, none more so than her father, stepmother, and Marion.

Many persons prophesied that the sorrow was too deep to last, the shadow too dark to linger very long; that Kathleen would brighten up; and that she who was, in one and almost the same hour, both wife and widow would, before the year was out, again exchange her name.

A nervous fever had laid her prostrate for several weeks following Leonard's death. With youth, however, and a naturally fine constitution, she rallied, and again moved about in familiar places, as of old.

Oh, have you ever felt your heart wither away, as it were, under some dire, crushing trouble?—have you ever felt the sorrow upon you through the death, or impending death, of some dear one, whom you would have saved with your own life, might he or she only be spared to you?—if so, you *can* imagine the depth of the sorrow which crushed her to the very earth. "Would she go mad under her calamity?" asked those who pitied and loved her; but no; reason was as unclouded as ever, but the shadow of her grief never passed away.

Then they reproved her, spoke of rebellion to the will of God, of a duty owing to others, of the strict necessity there was for shaking off this well-nigh despairing sorrow; but all in vain.

"I am not rebellious," she would meekly say, for all her native impetuosity was gone; "but let me bear in silence my great grief."

There was one, however, to whom she was now drawn by ties of a most tender love. Poor Mrs. Burke had taken the motherless sufferer, who had so often opposed an icy chillness to the overtures she had been prompted to make, to her own warm heart, and had at length found an opening to that of Kathleen. What was the talisman which gave her admittance to the sealed-up heart at which she had been knocking, knocking two long years without avail?

That talisman was named Adversity! It had come to Kathleen in the shape of death. But call it sorrow, grief, trouble, what you will, there it was; it comes to us all sooner or later—to some more is given, to others less. I know not if those who have less can safely be termed the happier of the two. Well for us, if we bear it quietly. The worst of it all is that we grow so very restive; young, and middle-aged, and old, we are all alike, ever, ever striving to shift from our shoulders this cross of ours. Could we but have any other, how much better we could bear its weight; and yet, as it is given us to bear, it needs must be the very best for us. But, you see, we do not see the gem concealed within its rough exterior, and so we are going on trying, trying all our life long to get rid of our shadow.

Well, I was saying that Mrs. Burke had at last the happiness of finding that she was loved—ay, and very dearly too; for the poor, forlorn girl, who in a few short hours had been at once maid, wife, and widow, felt as if she could never make up sufficiently for former little slights and coldness.

About this time Ellen took it into her head to tread in Minna's footsteps; yet not exactly so, for she would leave Rutland Square for a certain house of good Sisters of Charity, not very far from her own old home; and thus it was that Ellen's commencement of the novitiate was the reason for Marion's return to England.

The good Mr. and Mrs. Burke, however, would not part with her without a testimonial of their affection and esteem; so the lady made her a present of a valuable brooch, and Mr. Burke, who knew what her intentions were, presented her with a bank-note for one hundred pounds!

Marion was very sad when the day arrived on which she was to bid farewell to her good, kind friends; more sad than ever, when she pressed to her heart the young widow, who, with a poor attempt at a smile, said,—

"I do not know, dear Miss Craig, that the knowledge that you are settled in the lovely place to which you purpose going will not lure me from my own home during the ensuing summer, so we will not say farewell, dear Marion, let it be *au revoir*; and may the shadow of grief like unto mine never sadden your fair face."

"Ah, but I too have my shadow, Kathleen," thought Marion, though she said nothing; "and mine is the grim shadow caused by poverty and disappointed hopes."

CHAPTER XVI.

DO ROLLING STONES EVER GATHER MOSS?—THE TORQUAY LODGING-HOUSE.

BACK in England—back to the old familiar place; this going *back to the old place* comprises a great deal that is very sad and painful sometimes, as you well know, gentleman or lady reader, if you have left that old place with the hope of mending your health or your pockets. Ah, it is not at all a pleasant thing, I can promise you, this coming back, especially if you have left old scenes with the hope of doing better in the new.

As long as the world lasts there will be censorious, uncharitable people, who *must* find fault with their neighbor, and the way he manages his affairs; and, at the same time, these sort of people are the very last who will give him a helping hand, though they can make a dozen trite remarks—such as that of the *amiable* Rochefoucauld, who said that *"misfortune was but another word for imprudence;"* or the well-known proverb, "Rolling stones gather no moss," &c.

Well, you see, Marion had a little of this sort of thing to endure. She had been a bit of a rolling stone in her way; and there were some two or three self-styled friends who, having previously ridiculed the idea of her going to Ireland, and dragging old Mr. Craig with her, when she could as easily have got a situation in England, were now quite ready to find out that she had best have stayed at home, till she proved to them that she had really gathered a *little* moss, as she had a hundred pounds in her possession.

"And what was she going to do with it? surely stay quietly in London, and seek another situation."

"Nothing of the sort; my health is breaking under constant exposure to the weather. I shall buy a little furniture, take a small cottage in the country, let part of it, and give lessons; thus I can live comfortably, and support my father till better days shall come."

"All very foolish," growled the catechist; "you'll not be able to bear strangers about you when you get them. Suppose your father were to become very ill, or your own health should break up still more than at present, what then?"

"Ay, what then, suppose the moon were to fall from the sky?" laughingly rejoined Marion, though, annoyed at the discouragement given to her, she immediately added, somewhat gravely, "Do you not think it a better thing to encourage young people, than cast down their spirits by a thousand suppositions which after all may never come to pass? I may *not* succeed; if I do, I shall prefer a quiet country life to that which I must lead in London. Therefore, please don't imagine for me horrors which may never exist."

The end of it all was that, a fortnight after her arrival in London, Marion prepared for her journey into Devonshire, Herbert and Lilian having vainly endeavored to make her change her resolution, and, leaving Mr. Craig on their hands, retire immediately to Namur, as the good nuns had consented to receive her without a pension.

Marion, however, would not hear of it; the poor old man, half in his dotage, clung to her with a childlike confidence. Should she leave him, when perhaps a little, only a little longer endurance would settle everything without any interference on her part?

Poor Mr. Craig, he had overheard this offer, so kindly meant on the part of Herbert; he had heard, too, Marion's rejection of the offer; still he was uneasy, she might be over-persuaded, he thought; what if she should have tired of him? And so, when evening came, he sat apart thinking of the past,—of old days, when he was a rich man in Manchester—of his rash speculations, by which he had risked his large property—of the folly of which he had been guilty, in not drawing in his expenses whilst there had been yet time to retrieve his shattered fortunes—of the tremendous crisis, caused by the depression in the cotton trade—his own bankruptcy—and then of all the dark trying scenes of the last two years,—and he asked himself the painful question, Was he living too long for Marion? But no; he dashed away the thought as quickly as it had entered his head; his Marion was true as steel. He was confident she would not desert him in the evening of his days, to follow out her views just a little quicker. Herbert was very good, and Lilian was *his* Lilian as well as Marion; but Lilian is married, and cannot do in her husband's home just as she would do were she single; he should not like, he was sure he should not like, to live in the house of his son-in-law, however good he might be. Thus much, and a great deal more, the poor old gentleman had thought as he sat there beside the window, a few nights before they left London, with his venerable head bent down on his hands, buried in deep and bitter thought; whilst Marion, whose active mind never allowed her to be idle long, was busying herself in those various occupations which have to be made when about to leave home. At last her work was finished, the sunlight was dying away, tinting with its golden radiance the clear blue heavens, clear despite the London smoke, and shedding a bright crimson tint over the bowed-down head of her father.

"What makes him so *triste* to-night?" she said to herself; "he is seldom so quiet; and I have been so busy both with head and hands, I have quite forgotten my poor dear charge."

Then advancing to his side, and stooping down so low that her bright golden curls mingled with his silver locks, she kissed his brow saying,—

"What is the matter, papa? What makes you so sad to-night? Why, shame on me to have so long forgotten to talk to you."

"Nothing is the matter, love, except that my heart is very sad."

"And why sadder than usual?" she said. "I think we ought to be more cheerful."

"I am thinking about this change, Marion; Herbert is very good, but only a son-in-law after all. I feel my poverty now, Marion, more keenly than ever."

"What do you mean, papa? What has Herbert to do with us, or *why* should you feel our poverty more than ever? it has been much worse than at the present moment, gloomy as the future may be."

"It has thus much to do, child, that now, when age is creeping fast over me, I have to give up even the poor home I have enjoyed with you, and reconcile myself to seek a home with Herbert."

"With Herbert, papa! what *can* you be thinking of?" exclaimed Marion.

"Did I not overhear Lilian saying this very afternoon that she and Herbert wished I would live with them, and that thus you could get to Namur at once?" said the old man, looking up at his daughter with a something of anger in his face.

A sudden light flashed upon Marion; she was, however, much shocked at the utter want of intelligence now betrayed by her father, who had evidently taken it into his head that she was making prepartions to go into a convent, instead of to take him with her to Devonshire, and, throwing her arms around his neck, she exclaimed,—

"My dearest father, what can have made you

think that this idea of poor Lilian's would ever be acted upon? It was *her* wish, not mine. Why make yourself so miserable? Never have I been otherwise than cheerful and contented, leaving the future always in the hands of God; besides, do you forget that we both leave London together for Devonshire on Wednesday morning?"

For a moment the old man mused, as if striving to collect his scattered thoughts, then he placed his hand to his forehead, and suddenly his face lighted up.

"Ah, yes," he said; "I remember now, love; how very stupid of me to forget it. And here have I been making myself so miserable, because I thought you were going to leave your poor old father. Yet, darling," he added, a sorrowful look again passing over his face, "it is a sad, sad thing to keep you struggling on with me, instead of your being happy in your own way."

"You dear old father, will you be quiet, and let me talk?" said Marion speaking in the coaxing tone one would adopt when talking to a child. "I *am* happy in my own way; there, will *that* content you? I am quite happy at thinking that we are both going to the beautiful country. It is only you who will make me the reverse, if you take such silly ideas into your head."

Thus gently combatting with her father's infirmity, the good Marion soothed away his trouble; and the next day but one, early in the bright spring morning, they left London for Exeter, on the way to Torquay.

It had been a moot-point with Marion whether she should not have selected some watering-place in Lancashire—such as Lytham or Blackpool—as the scene of her future labors; but, on second considerations, she changed her mind.

You see she was no saint, this Marion that we are telling you about. I question whether, if in the end she does get to Namur, she won't find that there is a terrible amount of work to be done; for the plain fact was, she would not return to Lancashire lest she should come in contact with any of their former Manchester acquaintances, who had all of a sudden forgotten, when his bankruptcy took place, that they had ever styled themselves her father's friends, and been sumptuously regaled by him in his rich house at Bowden. It was very natural, you know, though not in accordance with Marion's standard of perfection, that she should feel in this way; but then, poor girl, she was so often below the mark. "Bad enough," she thought, "for those cold-hearted people to know that I have to give lessons; but more terrible still, were I to get them, or any of their friends, into my own house."

So it was, then, that she determined on removing to Torquay—a place to which she was quite a stranger, but of the beauties of which she had heard much.

Those who know the road between Yeovil and Exeter will bear witness with us as to the beauty of the scenery; but can there be a lovelier scene than that between Exeter and Torquay, with the noble sea and over-hanging cliffs greeting the eye at every turn in the road?

At last the journey is over; and, gazing from the window, Marion beholds, a little distance from the station, cliffs covered with creeping plants, and crowned with a cluster of white villas, hanging as it were between earth and heaven.

"What a lovely spot!" involuntarily burst from her lips; and lovely it was, especially viewed in the soft sunset of that fair May evening, the light fleecy clouds breaking here and there, and the clear blue of the horizon, dyed with its own gorgeous hues, shedding a golden light on the broad and beautiful bay.

For that one night Marion put up at the Queen's Hotel, facing which arose a cliff covered with the wild primrose and profusion of creeping plants.

Early in the morning she sallied forth to explore the place, and engaged a cheap lodging in the Avenue Road till she could meet with a habitation, which she very quickly found on the cliffs. It was a pretty cottage, affording just sufficient rooms for herself, her father, and a servant, and also for one family. This cottage she furnished in the simplest manner; but everything was neat and clean, so that her rooms did not stand long unlet, and even fetched a good price.

So far all was *couleur de rose*, and Marion's spirits were high; but of course her new life had its drawbacks, and she will find out what they are quite soon enough.

Marion was wholly inexperienced, had never been accustomed to have strangers about her before. It won't exactly do, she thinks, to take for a guide as to charges that hard woman with whom she had lodged herself in the Avenue Road. Marion considered her charges extortionate, and so they were.

"Would she not make a reduction in her bill?" Marion suggested, somewhat timidly.

"No; she should insist on the whole amount," which Marion paid with great disgust, considering herself imposed on, and no longer wondering that harsh things were said about persons who let their houses not being always very honorable; for the world, unhappily, views things *en masse* but too often.

Owing to her Catholicism becoming quickly known, Marion found it extremely difficult to get pupils, as she had expected, so that you see she was thrown rather too much on the little her house would do for her here; thus was the first shadow thrown over her path, in her otherwise pleasant home.

The once rich Miss Craig, too, could not so utterly forget the past as to *like* the employment which fell to her lot in the kitchen: she felt herself painfully above her present position; and though she strove perpetually to call to mind the humble employments of those privileged ones in the lowly house at Nazareth, still her sensitive nature shrunk oftentimes from the performance of such servile duties.

"Broken-down rich people!" Alas, alas, how much of human misery do not these words comprehend! Bad enough, hard enough, are the trials of poverty for those who have never known the comfort which wealth can bestow. Very trying is it to the poor lady or gentleman—the clerk, the governess, the artist or the author—to keep up that respectable appearance which they must of necessity maintain, for an outward share of respectability is all the world to them. And there are few who will deny that such as these have oftentimes more to suffer, and far more difficulty in getting employment, than the working classes, if the latter be but industrious and sober; for it is an undoubted fact, that persons who minister to what we may term the luxuries of those above them in a worldly point of view, have far more to encounter than those whose lot it is to contribute to their necessities. Take, for instance, the domestic servant and the accomplished lady, each in quest of employment. If the former be but industrious and civil, never need she lack a good situation; whilst hundreds of poor governesses and lady artists, with all the refined and delicate feelings which education bestows and strengthens, seek it oftentimes in vain.

But worse, far worse still than this, is the state of those who *have* been rich, and then by some hideous catastrophe are plunged in poverty, such as was that of poor Marion Craig. How much to learn, how much to suffer, how much of human feeling to subdue! We have said why she did not choose a place rising to notoriety, like that pretty Lytham, with its almost entirely Catholic population; honest, kindhearted Lancashire folks, who would have welcomed her so heartily amongst them. Well, I have told you why she did not go there; she was not quite humble enough to make up her mind to encounter the Manchester people, her own former acquaintances, many of whom patronise Lytham and Blackpool, and so went to Torquay instead.

Ah, Marion, Marion, all this rebellion of your proud heart is vain; for how true are those words of the author of that inimitable work, "The Following of Christ:"—"Dispose and order all things according as thou wilt, and as seems best to thee, and thou shalt still find something to suffer, either willingly or unwillingly, and so thou shalt still find the cross." So it was that one bright summer evening, just after the trains had come in, there was a sharp ring at the hall bell. The maid was asked what apartments were to let, and, with a burning flush suffusing her cheeks, Marion came forward and recognised an old acquaintance of her father's, accompanied by his wife and two daughters.

An exclamation of surprise burst from their lips; and then the painful question was asked, Were they staying at Torquay? how long had they been there? they were so glad to meet them again.

Come, Marion, it is surely time to lay aside your pride, for you must disclose the truth, and accept the humiliation which has come to you quite without your seeking for it; for you have wandered a great many miles from your old place, lest you should encounter any of those you knew in your rich happy home at Bowden; and yet here they are in Torquay, and, amongst many other houses with bills in the windows, have come to you after all.

A really kind-hearted family, though, were these Howards, and sorry did they feel that they had not at once comprehended that Miss Craig had come down so low in the world, as far as money matters went, as to let lodgings; so, affecting not to notice the confusion of this poor proud Marion, as she faltered out that her father and herself held the house, but that they let part of it off, they asked her terms for the ensuing month. On hearing which, the rooms were immediately engaged; and whilst they returned to the station to give orders about their luggage, Marion, smothering the sigh which rose to her lips, prepared for the accommodation of those who had once felt themselves honored by the acquaintanceship of persons who had been infinitely above them in point of worldly wealth.

There is no doubt, however, but that Mr. and Mrs. Howard would have passed by Torre Cottage, had they known who were its occupants. "There was something inexpressibly annoying," said the lady, "in the thought of that delicate, accomplished Marion having to cook and superintend things for them." There was no help, however, and before night they were installed in their temporary home.

To their astonishment, they were not many days in Marion's house before they discovered that an utter change had come over her. With a kindly wish to save her trouble, Mrs. Howard kept as plain a table as possible; but thoughtful Marion surmised the reason, and Mrs. Howard expressed her wonder, when several little delicacies occasionally appeared on the table, that the formerly rich young lady knew how to watch over the comforts of her lodgers better than that person in the Strand with whom she lived last year, and who had never occupied the position of a lady after all.

Mr. Craig's helplessness and imbecility, too, won their hearty sympathy. It was shown after their departure from the house in the shape of a hamper containing three dozen of choice wines for himself, and a token of friendship for his daughter. Marion had perforce made a step in advance; she would now as soon have any of the Manchester people as strangers—perhaps sooner; for they might exercise a little more forbearance towards her than the latter would be ready to do.

However, let us leave her for a while, merely adding, that there is nothing which brings not its own peculiar difficulties—and Marion gradually finds out what hers will be. She will not always meet with kind-hearted souls, chary of giving trouble, or with those whose minds are refined enough to treat with her as an equal. No; far oftener, poor Marion, will your delicate frame, so unused to such active employment, bend beneath the yoke imposed by those who will never think of sparing you;—far oftener, unless you become utterly dead to self, will your proud heart, owning its own weakness, fail, because you cannot brook being addressed as an inferior to those now above you as to worldly means.

CHAPTER XVII.

HOW HERBERT'S FIRST ESSAY WAS REVIEWED—A FEW WORDS TO YOUNG BEGINNERS.

SLOWLY, though surely, the Leslies beheld a break in the clouds that had hung over their fortunes, and a bright gleam shone through, revealing the silver lining beneath.

Mr. Richmond had proved himself a warm friend; had recommended others to Herbert's studio; and, moreover, had labored so strenuously in his behalf, that he had procured from a friend an introduction to one of the leading periodicals, and thus the first of Herbert's papers on the fine arts was already in type. For these he was to be paid a given sum weekly, which sufficed to remove them to a more comfortable lodging; and Lilian consoled herself with the hope that, at no very great distance of time, she should be able to release Marion from the hard life she was aware she was leading at Torquay; and, if her father should still cling to her sister as hitherto, she could at least, have the happiness of knowing that her own brighter prospects would help considerably to the amelioration of their sorrows; for she had determined that they should share one common home. Mr. Richmond had also let them into much of the manœuvring which, as in everything else, lies hidden under the surface in the literary profession; had bid him not be discouraged, but push energetically forward; telling him to remember that true talent never exists without a corresponding energy and perseverance.

At last the first portion of the article written by Herbert appeared. The *first!* and remember, O reader, how much depended on his success for the long future spread before him—either one of three things: a sort of mediocre success, which should snatch him from the misery which surrounded himself, his beloved Lilian, and her family, and establish his claims in some degree as a worthy claimant on public favor, both as an artist and an author; an utter failure, the result of which would be extremely hurtful to him in both capacities, and would even leave him worse off than in his original position; or a brilliant success, such as falls to the lot only of a favored few, and is too often not so much the result of any peculiarly striking talent as of some fortuitous chance, unusual good fortune, or even of some powerful interest, in a country in which so very little is accomplished, unfortunately, without it.

It happened, then, that on one pleasant September morning, just as Herbert was making his preparations for going to his studio, the first number of the —— *Magazine* was sent him, per post, from the publisher, accompanied by a couple of newspapers. He opened, of course with that nervous eagerness which a young author is sure to feel, the magazine in question ; whilst the delighted Lilian, her big black eyes beaming with pleasure, leaned over his shoulder; for not content with hearing Herbert read his article aloud, *she* needs must read it too. Then he opened one of the newspapers, feeling confident that he should there see, as indeed there was, a review of that article of his which he had just perused with so much delight. What did he see, however, but half a column pregnant with all that spiteful satire with which the reviewer's pen becomes envenomed when he wishes to *cut up*, as the term goes. Not only was poor Herbert's article abused through thick and thin in points perhaps where it might be justly assailable, but where praise ought duly to have been meted out it was withheld. He knew *nothing* of the subject concerning which he wrote; he was wrong on every point ; and the reviewer ended by advising him to study the matter at issue from its first elements before he should venture to put pen to paper again.

All know how that poor, talented creature Keats was affected by the lash of the reviewer ; how he allowed the unmerited abuse he had received to have such an effect upon him that it was the cause of his death ; how that noble Byron, gifted as he undoubtedly was, was treated by them, and how keenly he felt their spiteful abuse ; and as Lilian noticed the effect the atrociously false article had upon her husband, she dreaded what the consequences might be, remembering as she did how similar articles had affected those to whom we have alluded. Fortunately, just as Herbert's fit of anger had subsided into one of melancholy, she heard a double knock at the door, and immediately afterwards their kind friend Mr. Richmond entered the room, before whom she placed the obnoxious paragraph.

"Why, Leslie, you surely don't mean to let me see you cast down for a piece of low spite like that," he said, tossing the paper to the further end of the room; "I thought you too wise. Why, any person can see, from the wholesale castigation levelled at your work, that there is personal feeling at the bottom of it; one-half of these wholesale sweeping condemnations are emanations from the pens of disappointed authors. And, after all, the public really go so little by the reviews, many persons never troubling to read them at all, that they never do the harm you foolish young authors are so apt to imagine. If a reviewer is inclined to act gracefully, well and good; I suppose there never lived an author who was not glad to see a favorable review—it is natural it should be so. But you must get over this silly fit, Herbert; I shall advise you to lay aside the pen, if you are going to let your peace of mind be disturbed by every reviewer who may take it into his head to be spiteful."

"And do you really believe, Mr. Richmond, that a *thing*—a rascally article like that," said Herbert, pointing to the crushed paper on the floor, "is not calculated to do a deadly injury to the reputation of a rising author?"

"On my conscience, no," replied his friend,—"most emphatically, no; the very thing speaks for itself as the invective of some interested person whom you have perhaps unwittingly offended—not a fair review, calmly and dispassionately written. Come now, promise me before I leave you that you'll view such matters in their true light; these are rubs which you must expect in this fair-dealing, kindly world of ours, and if you take them in this way, I shall expect you will copy the example of that foolish fellow Keats, so that the sooner you lay aside the pen the better; I for one would not help you on your way."

"Oh, look here, Herbert; read this," exclaimed Lilian, who, whilst Mr. Richmond was talking, had had the curiosity to open the other paper, which her husband in his anger had thrown aside; "see, now, there is something here to make amends for all that tirade which has annoyed you so much;" and she forthwith read a very fair review, neither lauding Herbert's article up to the skies nor condemning with faint praise, but one which did justice both to the head and heart of him who penned it, and who concluded by wishing a God-speed to the efforts of the young author whose production bid fair for future success.

We will leave them for a while, first remarking that Herbert resolved to treat henceforth such articles with the contempt they deserve, and strive his best to win his way and earn public favor both by pencil and by pen; whilst Lilian builds up *chateaux en Espagne* for herself and Marion, wishing —oh, vainly wishing—that that dear, good Marion would content herself with leading a good life in the world, and not run away and leave her just when they might all be *so* happy.

Just one word, Miss or Master who may read our pages. Take warning by Herbert's anger and folly. This is a very hard world for young people to make their way in, and you will require great perseverance and industry on your part, whatever be the occupation to which you devote yourself. Even our very friends may sometimes be obstacles in the way ; for you know Holy Writ itself says, *"No man is a prophet in his own country."* And if you show any particular talent, never mind in what way, there will be many discouraging things said to you, the *young* beginner, who of all others need kindly and encouraging words. But never mind whether the obstacles come from friend or foe, so that your own conscience tells you you are right ; fight on, do the battle of life well, and you will surely succeed in some degree in the end.

Only be sure of one thing, and that is, that you are not fighting *in* the world if God calls you *out* of it—supposing always there be no impediment, such as want of health or discharge of filial duty ; and then, you know, whatever your desire might be, it may be taken for granted that after all the world is to be the sphere of your labors. Labor, then, therein faithfully and diligently,—never think of folding up in a napkin the talent God may have given you,—and set out with two things in your mind, which you must always keep in view—namely, that there will be much to discourage and cast you down—this you must strenuously fight against; secondly, that it is quite right, and in accordauce with the laws of reason and religion, for you to pursue diligently every lawful and just calling. Win your way honorably in the world if you can, acquire a place in society if in your power ; so long as you earn it by no dishonorable means, you have every right and title so to do.

CHAPTER XVIII.

STRONG PREJUDICES—LIFE IN THE CLOISTER.

"Now, Mrs. Bowring, this really is *too* bad," said Marion to a lady somewhat about middle life; "here you have been telling me you are going to stay six weeks longer than you had intended, because you do not feel as if you were in lodgings, and that everything has been conducted with so much honor as to your bills and other matters, and yet you will leave me with the uncomfortable impression that, had you known I had been a *Roman* Catholic, as you call me, you would never have come to live in my house at all."

"Oh no, my dear Miss Craig, my prejudices do not extend quite so far," replied the lady; "but it was a bit of a turn to me. I thought you an Anglican."

"But, my dear Mrs. Bowring," replied Marion, "your face has fallen to an angle of forty degrees since I told you the fearful news. Now, from any one of Low-Church tendencies I might have expected something of the sort, but not from a lady who uses our own beautiful book of the Imitation, and who approximates so closely to us as you do."

"But, indeed, Miss Craig," said the lady, who,

the reader must understand, had but just discovered Marion's Catholicity, "you do not know half the things which have come to my knowledge about the Roman Catholics. I am sure I cannot tell you what I have suffered since that self-willed girl of mine threw off her own faith ; however, she will be here in a few days, poor Maud ;" and here Mrs. Bowring sighed deeply. "*How* little I thought any child of mine would ever be a Catholic ;—but I was saying, Miss Craig, you don't know half as much as I know about them."

"Oh, how ridiculous, Mrs. Bowring," said Marion, with a hearty laugh ; "how very ridiculous to maintain that! I, baptized in the Church and reared in a convent school, do not know my religion as well as you do,—what *can* you be thinking of?"

"You are one of the deceived, Miss Craig," said the lady, with great gravity ; "you know not what awful places those same convents are. I like you *so* much that I am quite sorry you are a Roman Catholic."

"Ah, me! and all the little good I possess is owing to the Church's teaching—shame be to me that I have not put it to greater profit," said Marion. "But you quite astonish me, Mrs. Bowring; I should not have thought you so full of prejudice. I quite long to see Miss Maud ; though I suppose you will forbid me to hold any intercourse with her."

"Oh, no ; you may talk to her as much as you

please," responded the lady. "The harm is done now, but her father has disinherited her. Heaven knows what will become of her, unless I can lay by something for her. *She* is talking of a convent too. Well, I don't know where she thinks the money will come from; she'll get no pension from us, I am quite sure."

"Dear Mrs. Bowring," said Marion, "the charity of many of our sisterhoods would, if they believed your daughter called to quit the world, receive her portionless within their walls. But why do you speak so harshly of them, you who *can* know so very little save by hearsay, which speaks with so slanderous a tongue?"

"Oh, there now; my dear Miss Craig, don't defend their practices, pray. The idea of a parcel of young women shutting themselves up, and living unmarried, when it is only right and proper for every woman to be married; and then, if *half* one hears be true, this apparent aiming at a higher virtue, as they take it to be, only leads to after unhappiness, and to some sad"——

"Oh, stop, Mrs. Bowring," said Marion, placing her fingers to her ears, for she knew that the lady was about to utter that most grievous calumny so often put forth against the spotless purity of the religious state. "I cannot listen to you, if you are going to talk in such a way; for, my dear Mrs. Bowring, if it be possible that that which is in itself holy—and what virtue can be more pleasing to God than purity?—can by any possibility be pushed to too extreme a limit, then this might rather be said of the religious state than the reverse—to such an extreme point of nicety in thought, word, and deed is the love of the most beautiful virtue of chastity carried; but it always strikes me as strange that you Protestants do not attack with half such vehemence the strict enclosure maintained by some of our religious orders, or the implicit obedience of the whole being to the will of another, as you do this most untenable point of all."

"It is all bad, *very* bad, *dire* bad" said Mrs. Bowring, shrugging her shoulders; "and I cannot think how sensible young women, who might be such ornaments in the world, and make good wives, can take themselves off, and bury themselves alive in this way."

"But who shall say if these ladies would ever marry, if they were to remain in the world, Mrs. Bowring?" said Marion. "Excuse me, but you seem to think that every woman may marry if she likes; look around and tell me now, don't you think there is a deal of forced celibacy? therefore is it in my opinion a very good thing that some of our sex voluntarily embrace it; it leaves the field open for others, you see. And even if they did not do this thing which you think so dreadful,—go and bury themselves in convents,— depend on it they would not be likely to marry for all that."

"Ah, well, you'll never, my dear Miss Craig,

make me a convert to your way of thinking; and it is because I have learnt to like you very much that I am all the more sorry you are a Roman Catholic. Well," she said, as she rose to leave Marion's parlor, "Maud will be here to-morrow—make acquaintance with *her;* I should like her to know you, because I admire you, though I *don't* admire your religion."

Marion laughingly told her that she should profit of the permission she gave her, and should lose no time in cultivating acquaintance with Miss Bowring, the more especially as she was in some sort an outcast from her family.

On the following day Maud Bowring arrived at Torquay. She was an unaffected, amiable young woman, with little to boast of in the way of personal charms; but in her frank open countenance there was such an expression of good nature, that it made ample amends for the want of beauty.

Mrs. Bowring introduced her daughter to Marion, remarking that, as Miss Craig had the additional misfortune of being a Roman Catholic, and also was designing at some time of her life to enter a convent, she doubted not but that they would soon become the best of friends.

Now Mrs. Bowring really *was* partial to Marion; virtue always has a powerful influence with others; and this violently-prejudiced lady really admired Marion Craig, yet, by a strange perversity, never asked herself what influence it was that directed her daily actions, and made the governing principle of her life. How it was that she was always cheerful and contented under the toils of her hard, hard life—that she bore so patiently the infirmity of her aged parent—that, intellectual and highly accomplished, she could yet descend to the coarse drudgery of domestic life—feel her social position so different to what it ought to be, and yet not murmur. Poor Mrs. Bowring, she was so very prejudiced that she really could not bring herself to believe that the wonder-working power of religion could do this; that Marion—and, poor soul, she was no saint after all, but a weak, imperfect young woman—owed it to the governing influence of that faith which more than any other exercises a powerful control over the ordinary actions and daily occupations of its members. She was certainly, too, a *rara avis* in Mrs. Bowring's mind. "She is not at all what I thought very religious Catholics were," she would say to herself; "she is working very hard all day—first at one occupation, then another, flying about the house in the morning in her neat print dress, looking as pretty as she is good; then if I poke my head in at the kitchen door, there she is with her white hands kneading bread or making pastry, or cooking the dinner. Ah, by the way, there *is* a flaw in her character; for when she was frying our soles the other day, I ran in unawares, and I saw her flush up to the very eyes, as if she was ashamed of her occupation. There was a little pride there, I warrant me;— however, let me see, there in the afternoon she sits mending up and altering her dresses, and they are all the worse for wear too ; she has only had one new one since we have been here, and that was a cheap muslin which she made herself; and let me see, four, five, six weeks," said Mrs. Bowring, counting on her fingers. "Why, she has eighteen pounds from me ; she must have little to depend on, then, beyond what this miserable lodging-house brings her. But let me go on, I have got over the whole day but the evening, and her only recreation seems to me to be a walk about the cliffs with that poor, infirm old man leaning on her arm. Well, she *is* very good, no doubt. *I* could not bear quietly such a life, for certain."

No, indeed, Mrs. Bowring, I do not think you could ; but then there is a sustaining, a governing principle, as I have already said, by which persons like Marion live, of which you, poor lady, are quite ignorant.

And what was this, but that one necessary offering in the morning of the works of the whole day ; that holy remembrance which should exist in the heart of every faithful child of the Church, that no action is mean or little which is done for God. Yet, our Marion could blush when caught at any servile employment, as Mrs. Bowring had sagely remarked ; ah, yes, but don't be too hard upon her ; for, like you and I, who are often trying to be very good and as often fail, Marion, if weighed in the balance, would, good as she was, have been found wanting at times.

As might be expected, Maud Bowring and Marion soon became excellent friends, so much so that, the second evening after her arrival at Torquay, old Mr. Craig not being well enough to accompany Marion on her usual evening stroll, the young lady craved permission to go with her instead, and they wandered together to the beautiful rock walk overlooking the splendid bay.

The day had been very sultry; but a refreshing breeze had sprung up, and they rambled on for a long while, occasionally bending over the steep overhanging cliff to admire the beauty of the scene, and the gorgeous sunset, shedding a roseate and golden glow over the deep, blue waters of the bay, and then wandering on again, talking of their past, and what their future might be.

Maud, you see, had a shadow around her, spite of her father's wealth; it was a shadow which, unhappily, has stolen around many—unhappily, we say, only in one sense, and that because, in our boasted land of religious toleration, such things should never be; her shadow was the loss of her father's love, because she had joined the Catholic Church.

Maud knew not why it was, but she was wonderfully drawn to this new acquaintance, this Miss Craig, of whom her mother had spoken in several of her letters.

It was not long before she had begun to speak of the shadow which her adoption of the Catholic faith had thrown around her path; then of her wish to enter a religious house, but her utter ignorance how to set about the work, as also the kind of life led by those who entered the more contemplative orders, threw an insurmountable obstacle in her way.

"I can obtain you every information," said Marion, "if you will accompany me to Beausite, a pretty villa amongst the cliffs yonder," she added, pointing with her parasol to the spot she wished to indicate. "There lives in that villa the orphan daughter of a naval officer, who, with a great desire to become a religious, but with no means to enable her to take the customary pension required for her future maintenance, was resigning herself to plodding through life as a governess, when she mentioned her wish to a good priest then on the London mission; the result was, that she was ultimately admitted, portionless as she was, to a community of English nuns of high standing established in the Netherlands."

"And did she commence her novitiate immediately, Miss Craig, and after all return to the world?" inquired Maud Bowring.

"No, no, not so fast," replied Marion, laughing. "The good priest, who did his best to help her, knew well that sometimes a sudden fit of enthusiasm may lead persons to the cloister who have rather an attraction to the quietude and repose of such a life than a vocation for its self-denials, and therefore wisely restrained Miss Arlington's eagerness. He would, she thought, settle everything almost immediately for her reception, either into this convent or the Sisters of Notre Dame at Brussels; but he had left England; and weeks lengthened into months, till nearly a year and a half had elapsed ere matters were brought to a conclusion by his return home. Lucy had before this fallen into a weak state of health, but nothing could turn her from her purpose; she would still go. Perhaps change of air—above all, the life she so desired to embrace might conduce to her cure; at any rate, she would make her trial, and she accordingly left England, to return again, after many months passed in the novitiate, unable to remain on account of her broken health, but encouraging for twelve long years the delusive hope that she should succeed at some future time, perhaps in a milder and more active institute, but obliged at last to abandon it; yet still cherishing in her heart of hearts the fond and affectionate remembrance of the holy lives of the gentle sisterhood who had loved and tended her in the hour of sickness, and whose hands, ever open to succor the afflicted, have never forgotten to succor *her;*—but here we are at Beausite; now you shall hear what Lucy has to say on the matter—you could not have a better authority."

For one moment Maud looked up, as if irresolute, at the little white cottage perched upon the cliff to which they had ascended by means of an almost interminable flight of steps, then, just as Marion's hand was raised to push open the gate, she said,—

"Not this evening, dear Miss Craig; such an interview as you are about to procure for me should not be lost upon my dearest mother; will you let her accompany us to-morrow evening?"

"By all means," replied Marion; "the thought never occurred to me. We will turn our steps back this evening, and see if we can induce Mrs. Bowring to join us."

The following evening the lady, with very goodwill, accompanied Marion and her daughter to Beausite, in which place Miss Arlington was spending a few weeks on a visit to some distant relations.

Maud had expected to meet with a very young lady, forgetting that Marion had told her that more than twelve years had elapsed since Miss Arlington had left the novitiate; she was for a few moments, then, surprised to encounter a person perhaps about thirty-five years of age, bearing in her, notwithstanding, cheerful countenance the undoubted marks of ill health; dressed very simply, in short, as any lady of slender means would dress—not in close crimped cap, and coarse black stuff gown, and large rosary hanging at her side, but attired in a pale blue muslin robe, with a simple linen collar fastened by a small brooch; whilst her chestnut hair, wreathed here and there with a few white threads, was braided over her thoughtful brow, the index of a mind which, at least, spoke of frankness candor.

Miss Arlington, you see, eschewed singularity,

which, whatever certain persons may fancy, is never the accompaniment of an unostentatious piety; she was no admirer of the fancy which some devout ladies living in the world take into their heads, who dress like Religious, and think it a sin to don a colored ribbon or a flower.

In the days of her early womanhood, which she had passed in the cloister of Nazareth, the good sisterhood had taught her that it was always best to avoid singularity; so that when she returned to the world she only wore her black dress as long as it was doubtful what her future would be; and when the long lapse of years, and still no cure, told Lucy Arlington that that future must be spent in the world and worldly duties, she at once resumed the simple garb of any other lady in her own position in life.

Lucy was just the proper match for the strongly-prejudiced Protestant lady whom chance had thrown in her way.

Marion had repeated to Mrs. Bowring what she had told Maud on the previous evening concerning this lady; and Mrs. Bowring had gone full charged, resolved to attack Lucy on all those points which she considered most assailable.

O Lucy, Lucy, how *will* you get on? Do you not tremble at the thought of things which you can't explain?—so many things, you know, which Protestants are cognizant of, by some strange freemasonry, far better than *we*, the children of the Church.

Lucy knew immediately the sort of person she had to contend with, for the moment the necessary introductions had taken place the lady exclaimed,—

"I am very glad to see you, Miss Arlington, —glad to see any lady who has been in a convent, and had strength of mind enough to return to the world. I shall feel grateful if you will let my foolish daughter into some of your convent secrets, perhaps it will make her change her mind about leaving the world."

Lucy bowed, and with a smile expressed her willingness to give any information that Mrs. Bowring might wish for, as far, she said, as one particular order—that of the canouesses of St. Augustine—was concerned ; and this would form a general outline of every other order.

"Well, then, first of all, you cannot deny that everything is made enchantingly easy, in order to ensnare a number of enthusiastic girls, who, when too late, may repent of their folly in pronouncing those three irrevocable and shocking vows which are taken in the cloister,—you cannot deny this, to begin with, Miss Arlington," said Mrs. Bowring, whose face was flushed with exultation at her marvellous discovery.

"I do most emphatically deny it," replied Lucy ; "it is a preposterous assertion, reiterated again and again by persons without the Church, and as frequently denied by ourselves."

"Oh, but I *know* it is so," replied Mrs. Bowring ; "I have read articles in the public papers and in books, all of which assert the same thing."

"Well, my dear madam," said Lucy, "it is of no use, then, to ask me for information, if you already know more than I do myself. It is, unfortunately, but too true that the most false and shameless assertions are paraded against us in the public press, and equally true that persons are found credulous enough to believe them; and, excuse me; but also prejudiced enough not to believe what *we* have to say for ourselves; so between the two we have no chance of a fair hearing."

"Oh, well, I am sure I am always ready to listen, Miss Arlington; but really I *have* heard *so* much that is awful about these places, and read—not only in the columns of the public papers, but even in books written by persons who have taken the veil, and then made their escape—so much that is dreadful and revolting to common sense, that one cannot do otherwise than believe persons who do not merely speak from hearsay, but from their own personal experience. Poor things, they have been known to marry after leaving the convent, and then they have spoken of the fascinating and alluring arts which the nuns have had recourse to, and by which they were inveigled into so miserable a way of life."

"Very likely, Mrs. Bowring," replied Lucy; "we must not forget that amongst the twelve apostles there was a Judas—small wonder, then, that amongst thousands of women there should occasionally be found some false to their vows, and who, with falsehood on their lips, traduce the holy life which their virtue was too weak to follow. Again, you express your pity for these 'poor things,' as you call them. Now you would think it very dreadful, I feel convinced, and would refuse to continue acquaintanceship with any married woman who broke her marriage vows, and then gave her heart elsewhere, yet you think it right in the perjured woman to break the solemn vows she has uttered to live ever for God alone ; however, if you really feel inclined to listen to the truth, and will give me a patient hearing, I will just describe, as briefly as I can, all that came under my notice during my nine months' novitiate in the cloister in the Netherlands, to which I have already alluded."

"Oh, I assure you," said Mrs. Bowring, "I am quite open to conviction, Miss Arlington ; and shall be but too glad if the very unfavorable opinion I have always had of those odious institutions can be in any way changed ; and as to Maud," she added, "I am sure *she* will lend a ready ear."

Now Lucy Arlington very much doubted the truth of Mrs. Bowring's assertion that she was open to conviction ; but wishful to do good, if there was any chance whatever, she commenced as follows:—

"I entered the novitiate when I was in my twenty-second year, the pension, which was eight hundred pounds, having been freely abandoned in my favor. It was towards the middle of an intensely cold day in January, in the year 1850, that I arrived in the old-fashioned town of ——. I had journeyed by rail from Ostend, and a short twenty-minutes' ride in a fly brought me safe to the convent—an extensive building, surrounded on three sides by a spacious courtyard.

"I was immediately shown into the apartments of the prioress, a spacious room with uncarpeted floor; a long wooden table, a few rush-seated chairs, a couple of *prie-Dieux*, various pious prints adorning the walls, and several shelves filled with books, made, as far as I can remember at this space of time, the chief objects in the room.

"The prioress was tall of stature, with a pleasing expression of countenance, soft hazel eyes, and a winning gentle manner, which at once enlisted my affection. Doubtless our Protestant neighbors would have asserted that this beloved friend who had opened her heart to receive the portionless English stranger, was already laying her snares to entrap an enthusiastic girl, though in what way she or her community were to be the better for receiving one without the customary dower, it would be hard to say. However, it is certainly the case that, ere I was long in her company, I found her one of those persons to whom we are drawn by an irresistible impulse. Before I had been many weeks in the cloister, I was obliged to own to myself that though particular friendships were forbidden,—and a very proper rule too, by the way,—there would, nevertheless, be a little corner in my heart in which the gentle lady who had received me would hold perhaps more than her due share.

"Taking me by the hand after half an hour's conversation, she led me down two or three spacious corridors till we reached a gallery which gave ingress to the church, a beautiful little building, in the choir of which, unseen by the laity, the nuns could perform their devotions.

"Down each side of the choir were the stalls of the religious, and just at the entrance, one on either side, were those of the prioress and subprioress. The stalls were made of carved oak; and at the end of the choir, surmounted by a large crucifix, was a low screen of a kind of filigree-work of brass and iron, standing near which, one looked down into the beautiful little church beneath.

The church is a light and elegant building, the floor composed of black and white marble, the altar a fine mosaic, the whole of the back, up even to the dome, being composed of richly-variegated marbles.

"From thence the prioress took me through the convent itself, leading me down the choir staircase to the chapter-house beneath, where the pensioners, or young lady pupils, gay and fashionable girls, the daughters of the *elite* of Paris and Brussels, hear mass daily. To the left, as we left the chapter-house, runs a spacious corridor leading to the school, an extensive building under the same roof, yet apart from the convent, and forming as it were, two distinct establishments. However, the mother prioress turned her steps to the right, and we entered the cloister, a long and spacious corridor paved with squares of black and white marbles, and arched overhead. On the left hand were the various offices of the convent; to the right several pointed windows, similar to those we see in our English churches, looked out on the church beyond; whilst immediately before you lay the little graveyard, long since disused for a quiet corner in a distant cemetery, but in which many of the canonesses were formerly buried.

"I was then shown the noviceship, or apartment of the novices, a long room furnished with the greatest simplicity, similar, in fact, to that of the prioress, but boasting, for the use of the novices, an excellent piano from the firm of Broadwood & Co.

"This room looked out into the garden, about three acres in extent, and abounding in fruit and vegetables. Here the novice spends great part of her time whilst necessarily remaining under the jurisdiction of the novice mistress—in all no less a period in this convent than six years and a half, the first six months as postulant or candidate for the veil; then, if she perseveres, she receives the white veil, and becomes a novice, and at the expiration of one year pronounces her final vows, and still remains another five years in the novitiate. And I assure you, my dear madam," added Lucy, "that so far from there being any ground for truth in the ridiculous assertion, that young ladies are entrapped by the insinuating arts which novelists and the press speak so much about, on the contrary, nothing is left undone thoroughly to test the temper and dispositions of the novice, who is tried in various ways, in order to prove to herself and the community whether her desire to join them has proceeded from what is termed in the Church a vocation for the life in question, or is merely the result of a passing fit of enthusiasm. If the latter, she will scarcely remain to conclude the lengthened term of her probation, and should she do so, and be afterwards unhappy, certainly she has only herself to thank for such a calamity, for every precaution that human prudence and foresight can take *has* been taken to guard against the possibility of such an error; and if, on the contrary, she has a real vocation for the life in question, the trial she has to undergo in order to testify her fitness for the life she desires to lead, both for her own future wellbeing and that of the community, will not cause her to return to the world. Do you think, my dear madam," continued Miss Arlington, "that I have painted the novitiate in such glowing colors that a young lady would be likely to be entrapped now, because she stands in any danger of being petted and spoiled, and her little passions and failings—and the best amongst us, you know, have them—yielded to, instead of being thwarted and resisted in every possible way?"

"Heaven help us, Miss Arlington! *what* a picture you *have* drawn of the novitiate!" exclaimed Mrs. Bowring; "a nice time these poor things must have of it; why, I should turn out before I was three days in their novitiate."

"Well, I am only telling you the simple, unvarnished truth, Mrs. Bowring," replied Lucy,—"the truth, as I have seen it, as I have myself found it, as I have witnessed its effects in others; believe me, when I tell you that the novice, however great her intellect, however accomplished she may be, however rich or clever, is as a little child in the novitiate, in which she has to learn as it were the elements of the religious life; it is the cradle of humility and renunciation of self-will; there I have myself seen evil passions subdued, and the froward and self-reliant become diffident and meek. And yet do not draw from thence an erroneous impression, and imagine that the novice is necessarily unhappy because her evil tendencies are thus carefully watched and repressed, for a love for the state she wishes to embrace leads her on; she is full of fervor, and runs rapidly in a path where others would fear to tread; keeping before her eyes one truth—namely, that she has left the world in order to aim at perfection itself, and flies from its pleasures and allurements in order to unite herself more perfectly to God. So much for our 'fervent novice;' the slothful one will not stay out her novitiate. Certainly, I must admit, that there have been, unhappily, unworthy religious—women who by some strange fatuity have deceived themselves and the most vigilant of superiors, and such as these have ended by becoming

a torment to themselves and a scourge to holy but
unfortunate nuns with whom they were associated ;
at last, and I must say fortunately in some cases
for those to whom they have become a scandal,
they end their evil course by abandoning the
asylum they had themselves so deliberately chosen ;
and not unfrequently do we see that the first thing
they do is to break the vow of chastity. But I pray
you, Mrs. Bowring, to remember, as I told you
before, that amongst the twelve apostles there was
a Judas ; small wonder then that here and there—
and blessed be God such cases are indeed but rarely
heard of—an unhappy, sinful woman breaks her
vows, and then seals her infamy by inveighing
against the holy state she has polluted, and decrying
and calumniating those whose kindly admonitions,
uttered as long as there was any hope they would
be profited by, have ended at last in sharp but
necessary reproof. From such as these, from
women who have broken the holiest of vows, we
surely cannot look for aught but falsehood and
calumny ; it would be as wise to expect 'to gather
figs from thistles' as to look for anything else, for
such as these know in their heart of hearts that
they have rendered themselves even more the
pariahs of society than the fallen woman who has
broken her bridal troth ;—in the eyes of all,
whatever be their religious denomination, who
have a just appreciation of virtue, notwithstanding
the effusions of certain anti-Catholic writers who
—at times from utter ignorance, sometimes from

sheer malice—paint such a one as martyr, extol her as a heroine, and speak of her as the victim to what they are pleased to denominate 'Papal superstition.'"

"Well, Miss Arlington, I must say you are giving me rather a different idea than any I ever entertained before of convents," said Mrs. Bowring; "but I daresay you will think me very prejudiced if I tell you that I am afraid I shall never admire such institutions; I still think they are very hurtful."

"Very likely, my dear madam," said Lucy; "a quotation from Hudibras may be well applied in a case like yours,—

"'Convince a man against his will,
He's of the same opinion still.'"

"Never mind mama and her prejudices, Miss Arlington," said Maud; "I, you know, do not share them, so please let me know something more about yourself; give me a little account of how you spent your day. Did time hang heavily on your hands? was not the greater part of it spent in prayer?"

"Oh, dear no; it is a very mistaken notion," replied Lucy, "to fancy a nun all day long on her knees in her cell or in the choir. I will just give you as brief a sketch as possible of our daily duties. *Imprimis*," she laughingly commenced, "the morning call is at half-past three."

"Half-past three!" exclaimed Mrs. Bowring; "why, you're not in earnest?"

"Oh yes, but I am; and when you remember

that in many orders the nuns rise at midnight, we were certainly not hardly dealt by, though I grant you it was very penitential to turn out of one's warm bed on a bitter winter morning so many hours before day dawned; but the nun prays while the world is buried in sleep, and works as the day advances.

"However, as all the nuns are aroused before she who calls them gets to the novices' dormitory, and my cell was the last in rotation, I had, you see, a little longer for rest, and I sprung from my bed directly my lamp was lighted, or perchance I might have lost myself in sleep again; then we were all in the choir before half-past four, when the bell rang for the first portions of the Divine office, taken from the Psalter of David, with various lessons from the sacred writings; and if one fresh from the world was inclined to feel lax and slothful, it was enough to warm one into fervor, to look around on that goodly throng of white-robed women, some bending beneath the weight of years, others still in life's morning, with the black veil just partially thrown back, enough to disclose the countenances, so varied in expression, of those cloistered ones, who sang aloud the praises of the Most High whilst others were buried in sleep, or at that still, quiet hour awake to sin. However, I fancy matins and lauds must have been over about quarter-past five, for I think we went to our cells at a quarter to six, and we always had half an hour for meditation. First, then, we employed ourselves in our various duties—making one's bed, and putting one's cell to rights—till the bell rang for prime and tierce, which were followed by the litany of the blessed Virgin, and then by mass. Mass would be over about twenty minutes past seven, when the bell rang for breakfast."

"And a very welcome sound too, I should think, after all those long hours in the cold," broke in Mrs. Bowring;—"but I beg your pardon for the interruption; do tell us what you had for breakfast."

"Tea, and bread and butter," was the reply, "except on Friday mornings, when all who were in good health only took a cup of coffee; then each one proceeded to her work—some to the school, to teach the pupils; others to their work, whatever it might be, in the work-room, the music-room, the garrets, the kitchens, or whatever part might be assigned by the superior, and remained there till eleven o'clock, when all proceeded again to the choir for Sext and None, another portion of the psalter, leaving the choir about half-past eleven for dinner."

"Dinner at half-past eleven!" thundered forth Mrs. Bowring and Maud at one and the same time; "mercy on me, these are primitive hours!"

"Perhaps so," said Lucy, smiling; "nevertheless, I always found myself ready for the meal in question, I assure you; and if you feel at all curious as to how we fared, I will answer you simply, that was such as becometh the table of a religious, three times every week abstaining from flesh meat, but what we had was both good and sufficient; then, let me see," added Lucy, pausing a few moments to try and remember that which, looked back upon through long years gone by, had become vague and indistinct,—"yes, at half-past twelve we had recreation, during which time we walked in the garden, read, worked for the poor, knitted, and conversed,—I forgot until now to mention that, except on rare and especial occasions, absolute silence is observed." Here Mrs. Bowring heaved a deep sigh, at which Marion and Maud both laughed.

"I think," continued Lucy, "we returned to the choir at a quarter to three, then we sang vespers, after which there was another half hour for meditation, perhaps an hour again for recreation, and then we met again in the refectory for collation."

"Collation!—why, you took no tea, then?"

"True, we had not that light meal, usual in the world," remarked Lucy, adding, "then we met again for recreation and needlework, Compline, a short meditation, with examen of conscience, closing the day; so that each entered her cell about eight o'clock."

"Well, and this, then, was the end of the day?" said Mrs. Bowring. "I must own it was a mighty different day to what I had imagined. But did you not find it very monotonous?"

"Not one bit more monotonous than the life of any lady in the world may be said to be, if she be accustomed to remain quietly in her own house, and fulfil the duties of her state of life; and again, the time is so judiciously used, that there is a perpetual movement from one thing to another, so that neither head nor hand is likely to be overworked by intense application, as is not unfrequently the case with our worldly employments; added to which it is wisely ordained that each member of a religious community shall be employed according to any special gift or talent by which she may be endowed; for instance, if fond of painting or music, much time would be given to either one or the other, you would probably be placed in the school, and if gifted with a fine voice, it would very speedily be heard in the choir. The nuns, however, have their days of rejoicing and festival, their *fete*-days; not the commemoration of their birth, as in the world, but of their religious profession. The jubilee, or half jubilee, of a nun is, too, a day of particular rejoicing, added to which there are various occasions during the year, the particular epochs of which I now forget, when a little relaxation is wisely allowed, though the great duties of the day are never, on any account whatsoever, infringed upon.

"I have forgotten to mention the habit of the regular canoness; it is composed of the coarest white serge, with a picturesque looking rochet of white linen, with a habit of a finer white serge beneath it, for the rochet does not come down to the feet. The coarse serge, worn next the person, is as austere, I assure you, in a burning summer day, as the utter absence of fire in noviceship and work-room is during the winter, especially if it be a severe one."

"Oh, mercy on me!" said Mrs. Bowring; "you surely don't mean to say that the poor nuns have no fire in the depth of winter?"

"Yes, but I most certainly do," rejoined Lucy; "and it was somewhat penitential too. But you forget their vow of poverty, my dear madam, as well as that this order of the great St. Augustine is considered very self-denying and austere; remember, too, that the vow of poverty made by a nun allows her to use nothing superfluous or that can by any possibility be done without; she can receive no presents save for the community at large, her clothes are well worn and mended; she cannot be said to possess even her own habit or her own books, as at any time they may be exchanged for those of another, indeed *mine* is a word never heard in a monastery, *ours* being the term in fashion in these cloistered asylums."

"And, dear Miss Arlington, do tell me what you mean by the word cell—what sort of a place is it? it's a horrid word, I think."

"A tiny room, of dimensions just large enough to hold a very small bed, little larger than one's coffin will be, that is all, with sheets of serge, uncovered boards, a chair, a *prie-Dieu*, a table, a wash-hand basin and water-ewer, and a glass just large enough to enable a nun to fix on her veil properly, that is all; and yet, believe me, these cloistered ladies rise in the early morning far more refreshed than a dissipated lady of fashion when she leaves her bed of down."

"Are they not very dull?" asked Mrs. Bowring.

"Quite the contrary; *I* was not half a day in the convent before I was asked if I were of a cheerful disposition, as if not, 'My dear child,' said mother prioress, 'you will not suit us;' I found them, in fact, the very reverse of dull. Religion was put forth in a pleasant aspect. I was not amidst the Puritans of old; and the religious of the Catholic Church know that a deep-seated feeling of religion is not incompatible with a good flow of spirits—oh, no; believe me, I have heard full often a merry ringing laugh in that happy cloister, and have seen, on their various *fete*-days, the good nuns, old and young, like a throng of gay, light-hearted girls,—and why not? surely, if properly viewed, nothing but a sour asceticism would forbid a joyous spirit.

"I have forgotten, too, to mention that much charity is dispensed from the convent gate, and this not only to the poorer classes, but also to the *genteel* poor. Take it for granted, Mrs. Bowring, that this vow of poverty is good for their neighbor, at all events; and well would it be for England now, and England's genteel poor, who are unmercifully harassed and threatened with executions when their poor-rates fall into arrears, if there were now richly-endowed monasteries and abbey lands instead of poor-law unions; but John Bull lets his bigotry run away with his common sense, and does not see in his own ignorance how little he or the country has benefited by the change.

"I have not yet spoken of the vow of obedience; you will bear in mind that it is *entire* in the full sense of the word. A nun lives by her rule, and the superior is also guided by the same; her voice is but as the reflection of the rule, and she has to see that it is duly observed. You will, however, understand that they are perhaps, with scarcely an exception, the beloved and venerated friends of their attached community. They are elected by the votes of the Religious, in many orders *not* for life,—in the convent of which I am speaking only for three years at a time, though they may be re-elected. The presentation order is regulated much in the same way with many others, had I time to call them to mind; and a novice is always admitted to her religious profession in the same way—by the votes of the sisterhood.

"That which received me was a happy and united community, founded at the time of religious persecution in England, and when the penal laws were in full vigor. It has ranked amongst its inmates the daughters of several of the most influential of the English Catholics, and is rarely without one or more members of their leading families; and it is but due to them to say, that I found amongst them examples of the most exalted virtue—generous, kind, and charitable. I was perfectly unknown to them, till introduced to their notice by a mutual friend, merely as a young lady who, desirous of entering religion, had no means to carry that desire into effect, and was about to earn her maintenance by teaching. I met with the affection we generally receive only from attached and well-tried friends during hours of tedious sickness, and which, after several months spent in the novitiate, occasioned my return to the world, and was but the prelude to a very long and almost fatal malady. I remember now with gratitude the kind attention and care I received at their hands, care such as can rarely be bestowed in the world, save when persons have a comfortable competency; and," added Miss Arlington, her eyes humid with tears as she concluded her narration, "I have become familiar with many of these much-maligned ladies since then in England and Ireland and Scotland, and certain am I that all are leading holy and self-denying lives, of which the world knows nothing, or knowing, could ill appreciate the motives from which their actions proceed. I have, I think, but a word or two more to say, lest I should have misled you, Mrs. Bowring, by the idea that money has anything to do in the matter of after employment in the community; it has nothing. Had I taken two thousand pounds for my portion, it would still have been the same; I should have been, in all probability, placed in the school, in which ladies of birth and high position already taught, who had taken their fortunes to the cloister."

"I thank you very much, Miss Arlington," said Mrs. Bowring, "for the information you have so kindly given me; though, I suppose, the effect it will have on my daughter Maud and my friend Miss Craig will be to make them more anxious than ever to become nuns, unless, indeed, you have frightened them by what you have told us about the trials of the novitiate."

Marion and Maud only laughed at the idea, Miss Arlington saying,—

"That is not at all likely to be the case, Mrs. Bowring. The young ladies, we must presume, seek a cloister in order to aim at a higher state of virtue than they might perhaps attain in the world; and will not be afraid of seeking it by the way of penance and self-denial, remembering the words, *'Take up thy cross, and follow Me.'* "

The harvest-moon was just beginning to rise, shedding its pale silvery beams over the distant cliffs, and lighting up the little parlor in which the ladies were seated. It was a moment for thought and reflection, when the busy tumult of life was over for a time, and the passions hushed and subdued. Mrs. Bowring was wrapt in a reverie; Marion and Maud were meditating on the future that lay before them; Lucy inwardly praying that the seed might take root, and that some of her simple, truthful words might have touched the heart of her very prejudiced hearer, and at the very least work for good in her daughter's behalf.

After the lapse of a few moments the lady rose

to take her departure, shook Lucy warmly by the hand, and bade her farewell, telling her she should be very glad to see her in Exeter, adding,—

"I will just own the truth—you have softened down my prejudices a little. I really did not think, from all that I have heard, that the nuns lived such lives as you describe; but then, you see, I never met till now with any one who had been in a convent."

Ah, and how many are there who think and speak like Mrs. Bowring, imbibing all their prejudices from the calumnious writings of such women as Henrietta Caracciolo and Maria Monk; and yet they are good souls after all, open to conviction, should they happily meet with any one able to inform them on a point upon which they have been all their lives most cruelly misled; for never have they had it placed before them that our Lord himself bequeathed these counsels of perfection. So it is, so it will ever be; there is no human institution under the sun which may not have its abuses, and be abused, either from faulty members within, or a calumnious world without. And the history of past ages, the records of days gone by, and also our present experience prove to us the truth, that there is no state so holy, no system so pure, but that scandal may creep in; and that there is no way of life, however exalted, which the harshly judging world will not decry and condemn, forgetting the words, "*Go sell what thou hast, and follow Me.*"

CHAPTER XIX.

THE SHADOWS OF THE GRAVE.

THE little party enjoyed their homeward walk as they descended from Beausite, the moonbeams touching with their silvery rays the trees and shrubs, and playing on the calm waters of the bay. Mrs. Bowring was unusually taciturn, and Marion could not help thinking that Lucy Arlington's simple narrative of her own experience as to convent life had had some little influence on the good lady's mind. They had returned home in good spirits; Marion hastening immediately to her father, who had been left unusually long to himself, save by the occasional visits of the servant, who told her that when she last entered the room he was asleep. Marion entered gently, fearing lest she should disturb him, and stood for a moment beside the couch mournfully contemplating the change in his features, a change traced more by sickness and care than by the hand of time. She had started as she stood beside him, so unusually ghastly did his always pale features appear, lighted up as they now were by the silvery light of the moon. He was breathing lightly, so lightly that she bent low enough for her hair to rest upon his brow before she could catch that faint gasping breath, and satisfy herself that the sickly, ghastly hue of his countenance was *not* the impress of death.

She drew gently away, the fears which had paralysed her had passed away, and she was stealing softly from the room when she heard him speak, murmuring her own name; she drew again towards the bed, believing him to be awake, but found him rambling in his sleep, and the following words fell upon her ear:—

"Yes, it is very hard work, hard work to struggle on; but the end will come. Yes, I have been selfish and worldly in the days that are past, and Marion, dear child, has been the sufferer; but she will have her reward, and I shall not be with her much longer."

All was again silent, but the sleeper turned uneasily on his bed, and Marion, unable to keep back her blinding tears, still lingered, not liking to leave him by himself. Then there was a struggle, as if the hard breath would only come with so much difficulty; and as Marion stood yet irresolute whether she should not call for a light, the stifling gasp again seized the sufferer, and noting the agony he endured, she tenderly passed her arms under his head, with the idea of relieving and arousing him from his painful slumbers at the same time.

Was it really the shadow caused by the pale and fitful light of the moon, or was it the gray shadow of death, which imparted to her father's countenance that deathly hue? yet surely never had Marion seen the rays of the moon impart so ghastly a tint before. And now alarmed, fearing the worst, though scarcely daring to express it to herself, she withdrew her arm with the intention of calling for assistance; but no, she cannot leave him, though the face becomes more rigid, and the eyes, preternaturally bright, are fixedly gazing on the daughter of his love; he bids, he implores her not to leave him, and his cold hand grasps her own with a tenacity which death only will relax; whilst the words, "Bless you, bless you, my own dear Marion," fall like an icebolt on her heart. "Nay, do not leave me; I am sleepy, darling; let me sleep. So, so," he said, laying his head upon her bosom. "Pray for me, Marion, my child; but do not leave me." And so, still rambling on in broken, incoherent sentences, he fell asleep; and that sleep was the sleep of death.

For a few moments Marion stood irresolute. Did he sleep? did he really sleep again? and bending down her head, she listens to catch the faintest breath; but no, she listens in vain. O God, could she but hear once more his querulous chiding as of old; then she bends forward, and kisses the marble brow, damp with the sweat of death. She knows the fatal truth; the silvery beams of the fair harvest-moon, shedding a refulgent radiance on all around, play upon those fixed and rigid features, on which no so soul could look and fail to know that the angel of death had spread his wings over that still, quiet form.

She knows the truth now, there is no longer room for doubt; she gazes for a moment horror-stricken, full of awe, on the features of the dead; and then staggering to the bell-rope, and pulling it with frantic vehemence, falls senseless on the floor.

Mrs. Bowring, alarmed at the violence with which the bell had been rung, was the first to enter the room, followed by her daughter and the maid. One glance at the silent form on the bed, and then at the prostrate figure of the unconscious Marion, told her the truth; and kneeling beside her, she raised her head, applied the usual restoratives, called her her "own dear Marion," reminded her of the lost one's pains and infirmities, and strove to soothe with those kindly offices which strike home to the hearts of the trouble-minded.

At last poor Marion recovered; and then, first dragging her weary limbs to the bed, she knelt down to pray for the soul's repose of one so dear to her, who after many long years of free-thinking had but since his residence in Torquay made his peace with God.

Then she insisted on herself rendering the last sad duties almost unaided. And with her own hands covering the face of the dead with a sheet, having first bedewed it with her tears, she went to her solitary little parlor to think *"how* she should bury her father."

"Charity never faileth," Marion; it is one of the works of mercy to bury the dead.

"First, there is poor Lilian to write to," she

says to herself, as she places her writing-desk before her and begins to scrawl, almost unintelligibly, a few hasty words, but pauses and shudders as she thinks of the *thing* overhead, no longer of this world; then she remembers that she must have black wax and black-edged paper, and she pulls the bell with such haste—so unlike to her own quiet, gentle way—that Maud runs in, in fear lest the hour *"by herself,"* which she has begged to have, should have ended in another swoon.

But no. "I am quite calm, dear Maud," she says,—her soft eyes raining showers of tears, by the way, quite contradict the truth of her assertion. "I will write to dear Lilian on this paper, and put it in a black envelope when Martha has purchased some;" and then again alone, and almost blinded by the tears which blister the paper as she tells her sad news, she finishes her letter to her sister; but bethinking that the evening post is out three hours since, she calls to Martha, and sends her with a message to the telegraph office, so that Lilian, if Lilian indeed have the money to travel with, may be there to-morrow night.

Three letters Marion wrote to persons whom she thought would help her in her heavy trouble, one of these was to Lady Evelyn, the lady whom she had been told had remembered her in her will.

Then, about eleven o'clock, she went to her room, first creeping in, in her loneliness and sorrow, to the bed of death. She had paused at the door of the chamber, shuddering at the thought that she was about to enter that room alone, then she reproached herself—"What could hurt her there?" Is it not strange that we thus feel awe-stricken at approaching those whom we have so loved in life? "It is a sacred duty," she says, "to look again on his dear features before I go to rest;" and then she softly opens the door and passes into that dread presence, kneels while she breathes a *De Profundis* for his soul, withdraws the sheet, and presses her lips on the marble brow, reverently replaces it, and steals shudderingly away, to pass a sleepless, tearful night of nervous wakefulness, keeping her light burning from a childish fear even of the ghastly moonlight; and, shall we own the truth? glad that Martha tapped at her door, and with pale face and trembling form asked, "would Miss Craig allow her to pass the night in her room, she felt so nervous and frightened like?"

The presence of the girl, who soon forgot everything in slumber, was nevertheless a comfort to the solitary mourner, and about daybreak she wept herself to sleep; but the horrors of the dread awakening—ah, those only can tell what they are who have suffered very deep grief, it rushes so upon us as we open our eyes to our renewed suffering.

At eight o'clock she heard the postman's knock; the letter was for her, and bore the Manchester postmark; she tore it open with trembling hands;

it was from Mr. Gilmour, and it told her of the death of her good friend Lady Evelyn.

She sat for a few moments transfixed with this fresh blow; her letter was now on its way, asking for assistance from her who, five days since, had paid the debt of nature.

Then came the natural thought—Was Mr. Gilmour's information correct? if so, she is gone whose generosity would have helped to smooth his passage to the grave.

Shall she ask Mr. Gilmour to aid her, should her other friends fail? The good-natured Burkes would receive a letter the next morning, also the gentlemen whose daughters she had taught at Clapham.

Yes, try him, Marion; he has a large family, but he is tolerably well to do in the world; perhaps it will please him to have a part in paying the last token of respect to the memory of his old friend.

Then Mrs. Bowring called for her on an undertaker, arranging about all those painful details which it was Marion's lot to discharge. And very wearily the hours passed away, till Herbert and her own darling Lilian made their appearance in the evening.

They had a little money, not much, but just a few pounds. "It would help to bury dear papa, love," said Lilian, as she stood weeping beside the still uncoffined remains; "and Herbert is sure to get on soon—we can manage." Marion had just five shillings in the house, that was all, and Lilian had forgotten, as she threw her seven pounds into Marion's lap, that they should all want mourning, and sighed heavily as Marion reminded her of this expensive requirement, but added, "Mrs. Bowring has called on a draper in the town, Lilian, he will send all that we shall require in the morning, and I can pay him as soon as I get the money."

Yes, "blessed are the merciful." Marion was not forgotten in her great affliction, for Mr. Burke and Mr. Gilmour each sent her a check for ten pounds, and her Clapham friends sent her five, and material for her best dress, so that the great trouble caused by want of money was spared them; and ever striving to save, the two sisters worked very hard to make up their own mourning.

And at last the day arrived when the remains of the once rich Mr. Craig were laid in a simple grave in the Torquay churchyard, the sisters and Herbert taking care to purchase the spot, so that it should not be opened for any other person; and a little later, when Herbert and Lilian were better off, they raised a small marble cross to his memory, on the face of which were the only words,—

"Of your charity pray for the soul of Archibald Craig. Aged 78."

Requiescat in pace.

CHAPTER XX.

FAREWELL.

EIGHT weeks have passed away ; Torquay has lost its charm now for Marion, Lilian and Herbert have been obliged to return to London, the furniture of the cottage is going to be sold by auction, and Marion will shortly go to Namur.

The bubble has burst, the will-o'-the-wisp, which, like an *ignus-fatuus*, lured Marion on, has turned out to be either a mischievous invention, a gross falsehood on the part of one to whom Marion was perfectly unknown save by name, or, if true, then Lady Evelyn, venerable in years, and long an invalid, had revoked her charitable intentions in Marion's favor, and expunged her name from her will at a later period. "Troubles never come alone," says the old adage. You see death was not the only one she had to contend with ; it was such a fine thing for a young woman who had not a *sou* in the world to look to, to hear that on the death of an aged lady there would be two thousand pounds for her to receive, that she could hardly be blamed if sometimes she had encouraged a hope that the story was true ; nor could she resign all hope, till a friend had applied to one of the executors, who speedily informed her that Miss Craig's name was *not* mentioned, in any way whatever, in the late Lady Evelyn's will.

"Well," thought Marion, "I suppose trouble is making me very apathetic. I could not shed a single tear at my disappointment now."

It was a good thing that this was the case. Excess of trouble sometimes seems to paralyse, as it were, our mental faculties, so it was with Marion ; her speculation at Torquay had been an unfortunate one. So that whatever her furniture realised would have to go to clear various little outstanding debts, and thus the nuns would have to receive her entirely empty-handed or not at all. There was no doubt but that in this case of Marion's, as in many others, the convent would not be benefited by receiving a novice whose affairs, in a pecuniary point of view, were in so terrible a predicament.

The evening before the day fixed for the sale of poor Marion's goods and chattels she spent with Maud and her mother at their new lodgings, and they accompanied her in the farewell visit she was about to pay to Miss Arlington.

Marion had observed that the prejudices of Mrs. Bowring had subsided wondrously since the meeting with Lucy ; so great is the power of truth, if the ignorant and prejudiced could but be brought to listen to it. The meeting was somewhat melancholy, as might be expected, for Lucy had learnt to love the patient, unrepining Marion. This, too, was the last time most probably that they would meet on earth, so something may be allowed for human feeling ; and you know, reader, as well as I do, *how* hard it is to say that one word farewell, to look your last, and then tear yourself away from one you have fondly loved. Well, this falls to the lot of all of us sooner or later in our path through life, even before the great separater, death, tears from us those whom we have dearly cherished.

The moment came at last ; Marion was the first to rise, when Maud exclaimed,—

"Dear Miss Craig, you were telling me that Miss Arlington had written some verses about that convent in the Netherlands ; do not forget that you promised to ask for a copy of them."

"I have a mind to scold you, Marion, for talking about my poor attempts at verse," said Lucy ; "they are not worthy to be paraded forth I know not where."

"Nonsense, Lucy ; let Maud have them at once," said Marion. "Who knows, some one of these days Mrs. Bowring may yield her consent," she added, with an arch glance at that lady, "and Maud may go tripping off to this convent of Nazareth, so much endeared to you. The cloister of Nazareth, what a pretty, sweet name," she continued. "If they would have taken poor me in your place, Lucy, I should have liked to make that my haven of rest; but that Namur, dear Namur, is waiting for me."

Lucy yielded somewhat reluctantly to the wish of her friends, and disappearing for a few moments, returned, bringing with her a copy of the following simple lines :—

"To the cloister'd shades of a quaint old town
  Come roam for a while with me;
Let us leave to-night fair Albion's cliffs,
  And pass o'er the deep blue sea.
Yon eastern sky, like a wave of gold,
  With a tinge of the ruby bright,
Foretells the approach of the summer morn,
  And chases the shades of night.
The breeze as it sighs o'er the smiling fields
  Draws sweets from the fresh-mown hay,
And seems to murmur and laugh with joy
  At the birth of the coming day.
The violet pale, 'neath its bed of moss,
  With perfume embalms the air;
And each drop of dew on its bright green leaves
  Seems like to a pearly tear.
The lark ascends, with its tuneful lay,
  To the firmanent on high,
Where the glorious sun now bathes with gold
  The blue of the azure sky.
But we will away from the woodlands green,
  From the rich and smiling vale,
Where each stream, like a thread of silvery light,
  Flows brightly o'er hill and dale.
We'll wander around the quaint old town,
  Where all is quiet and calm,
While the sunbeams play like lambent flame
  O'er the towers of Notre Dame.
The dazzling light through the rich-stain'd glass
  With the rainbow's hue doth vie,
As it gleams o'er the tomb where Charles the Bold
  And his fair young daughter lie.
But now let us hie to the convent fair,
  For the nuns at early dawn

Intone the praises of Him who doth give
  Both night and rosy morn.
Above earth's goods and its fleeting joys
  Their cloister'd state they prize;
And their voices sweet, like incense rare,
  Towards heaven now gently rise.
Look at yon aged and feeble nun,
  She was once a maiden fair:
With diamonds clear as the snowdrop pure
  She entwined her raven hair.
In beauty of mien none fairer than she
  E'er graced the festal hall;
The charm of her fair and beauteous face
  Was the gem of her father's hall.
But her heart was far from earth's vain joys,
  In the peaceful cloister's shade,
And without a sigh or a pang of regret
  Her last adieu she bade
To the world, that was void and naught to her;
  And now, a white-robed nun,
She lingers till God shall summon her hence
  When her earthly course is run.
Fair is the cloister of marble white
  When lit by the moon's pale ray,
Or bathed in a flood of golden light
  At the close of the summer day.
Beneath its arch'd windows doth lie the spot
  Where those who from earth have fled
Now sleep, while the zephyr doth gently sigh
  A requiem o'er the dead.
The church beyond still glows with the rays
  Of the glorious setting sun,
Now sinking midst waves of purple and gold,
  For his daily course is run.
The sisters are singing their Compline hymn
  At the close of waning day;
Sweetly their voices mingle and blend—
  Now swelling, now dying away.

> Fancy full oft waves her magic wand,
>   And I seem to roam again
> 'Neath those cloister'd shades,
>   For that much-loved spot
> Will memory e'er retain.
>   Through the marble cloister I pass once more,
> Greet fondly each sister dear;
>   'Tis fancy, but oft in the hour of prayer
> They seem to hover near.
>   Farewell, and may Heaven's choice gifts descend
> O'er novice and gentle nun,
>   May God's bright light be their evening star
> Till His own eternal Son
>   Shall summon them hence to the realms above,
> Where the depth of God's bounty lies;
>   For eye hath not seen, and ear hath not heard,
> What lieth beyond the skies."

Lucy's simple verses were read and duly admired by critics so gentle as the ladies in question; and then the farewell, that odious word farewell, was at last pronounced, and Marion and Miss Arlington parted *for ever*, for their paths in this world would be widely apart from each other.

The next day was spent amidst the horrors of a public sale, the following in settling various debts with the proceeds which had accrued therefrom, and the last days of Marion's residence at Torquay were passed with Mrs. Bowring and her daughter Maud.

It was on a fine September morning that she looked her last on that lovely spot. She was now about to enter on the state of life to which she had so long aspired; all the future seemed to her as bright as the sunrise which gilded the summits of the cliffs, shedding its roseate tint over the broad waters of the bay, and brought out the varied hues of the luxuriant foliage of the trees which cluster thickly around the pretty roadside station.

Though, as we have said, a pleasant vision swam before the eyes of the much-tried Marion of future peace and happiness in the state to which she had so long aspired, her spirits were nevertheless depressed. She had risen with the dawn that bright morning, and before any one was stirring she had passed through the fields and lanes leading to the church-yard, and while the pearly dewdrops still gemmed the grass she had stood silently weeping and praying by the humble grave of the *ci-devant* rich millocrat.

Then, too, she had passed through scenes well calculated to depress; the sudden shock of her father's death, his loss, the very time which she had been used to devote to him since he had been so long an invalid seeming to hang heavily upon her hands,—all had contributed to cast a shadow over her, which she could not shake off until she had been some hours on her way to London.

Arrived at the station of the Great Western, she there met Herbert and Lilian, who had removed to Hampstead, and with them she was to pass the few days which she intended to give to home and home ties before she broke them for ever by leaving England for Namur.

During the intervening time she managed, however, twice to visit her old friends at Canley, not a little to the regret of the affectionate Lilian, who could not bear her out of her sight, so short was the time she now intended to give to the world.

"Will nothing shake your resolution, my dearest sister?" said Lilian; "are we to lose you for ever? Herbert's studio, no longer in that dull, unfrequented street in Soho, is now often thronged by those who can pay him well; and his essays on the fine arts have made some sensation, notwithstanding the spiteful reviews he received at his outset, and the efforts made by envious and interested persons to throw obstacles in his way. Happy should we be, my sister, if together we might form a loving and united family, for Herbert now has a promise of enough and to spare for all of us. Give yet three months more to consideration, Marion, ere you cast a dark shadow over my future by this voluntary separation. Ah, grant a little to the joint efforts of Herbert and myself to retain you with us!"

"It may not be, my own dear Lilian," said Marion, gently disengaging herself from her sister, whose arms were twined around her neck. "Let not your love for me, my own darling, prove prejudicial by seeking to turn me from the resolution, not of days or months, but formed years since, when we were happy girls, and reputed rich in this world's goods; no, my Lilian, rather pray that I may be faithful to *my* vocation, as you have been to yours,—let me hope to be a happy nun, devoted to the service of my God, even as you are a happy and devoted wife."

Lilian never touched more upon a subject alike painful to herself and to Marion. Herbert, too, had done all he could to turn her from her purpose, and the next evening they stood with her on the deck of the steamer which was to convey her to Belgium.

We have little more to say, for we have heard that she has passed through her novitiate, and uttered those vows which death alone can break, and will shortly return a happy nun to dear old friends in the convent at Canley.

Lilian and Herbert are doing prosperously in the world; he is spoken of as a rising artist and author, and his beautiful Lilian as a model English matron, in these degenerate times. There is a shadow in their paths, for their union has been unblessed by children since they lost their firstborn, Archie.

It is quite true, though, that there is scarce a home in a thousand without a skeleton; whether people are willing to admit its existence or not, there it is, in some shape or other, the necessary alloy in all earthly happiness, preventing us from being too much wedded to the world, as mayhap we might be were there no shadow here below to mar the bright sunlight around us.

Perhaps, reader, we shall see hereafter, when we are touching the confines of eternity, that it was well for you and myself that we each had a skeleton in our house, for so I term our worldly crosses—those which are not brought upon us by our own sin or folly.

We have heard that Minna Sheldon, Mrs. Burke's daughter, persevered in her vocation, and is now a professed religious; but that Ellen made a mistake, the novitiate proved that she *never* had a vocation; she left after six months' probation, during which she tried both her *superiors* and *herself;* three months since she became *a wife!*

Mr. Burke has paid the debt of nature; and Kathleen, her shadow ever by her side, but quiet and resigned, is now seen to move about with some little of her old sunny smiles; her faithful friend and stepmother resides with the young widow; and Mrs. Burke, with the hope of seeing her become more cheerful, has purchased a handsome house near to the home of Lilian, with whom they have become very intimate. Mrs. Bowring's prejudices are wondrously softened since her conversation with Lucy Arlington. Maud is very intimate with the latter lady, and hopes at a future day to make acquaintance with the inmates of the cloister of Nazareth.

Let the curtain drop, reader, for our tale is ended. Happy is the writer, if some one of the very many who are so terribly incorrect in their judgments as to the point on which we have written, should read these simple pages, and accept the truth we have striven in our poor way, and from our own experience, clearly to illustrate—

namely, that the novitiate is no trap to ensnare and allure enthusiastic girls, but rather a time granted for cool deliberation, for earnest and searching trial; and in which, if there ever *be* such a thing as a mistake committed, it most assuredly rests with the obstinacy of the individual, rather than the slightest fault in the conventual system.

Happy those who fulfil worthily their *respective* vocations; for most assuredly hath God called some to serve Him in the world, and others in retirement: *the Spirit breatheth where He will.*

[THE END.]

KELLY, PIET & CO.
Printers, Publishers,
BOOKSELLERS, STATIONERS,
AND
Importers of Foreign Books,
174 BALTIMORE ST., BALTIMORE,

Have the pleasure to announce that they have completed the improvements in their building, which has been fitted up with every convenience to meet the demands of the varied departments of their business. They have now on hand a complete stock of

CATHOLIC BOOKS,

Which embraces, independent of their own Publications, all the Publications of the AMERICAN CATHOLIC PUBLISHERS, together with a large assortment of

European Editions of Standard and Approved Works.

Their Stock in the line of RELIGIOUS ARTICLES is well selected, comprising

Pious Engravings, Rosaries, Medals, Statues,
CRUCIFIXES, HOLY-WATER FONTS, Etc., Etc.

They keep constantly on hand a large supply of

SCHOOL and TEXT-BOOKS and ALL SCHOOL REQUISITES
Used in Schools, Academies, and Colleges,

Together with a select stock of

MISCELLANEOUS BOOKS,

In the various departments of Literature and Science, and all New Works as soon as published. Also a well-selected Stock of

CAP, LETTER, and NOTE PAPERS, and STATIONERY GENERALLY,

All of which they are prepared to sell at very low prices, Wholesale and Retail.

Steam Book and Job Printing.

The PRINTING DEPARTMENT, occupying the upper stories of the building, is supplied with the latest improvements in Type and Machinery, and in charge of experienced workmen under their own immediate supervision, enables them to execute orders with Neatness and Dispatch, at LOW PRICES.

They have a well-arranged BOOK-BINDERY, and are prepared to do every variety of

PLAIN and FANCY BINDING and RULING

Upon the most reasonable terms. ACCOUNT BOOKS of any pattern of ruling made to order. Their long experience and thorough acquaintance with all the details of the different branches of their business, render them confident of being able, and they are determined to use every effort on their part, to give entire satisfaction to all who may favor them with their patronage.

☞ ORDERS are respectfully solicited, to which they will give careful and prompt attention.

KELLY, PIET & CO. will send by Mail, free of postage any of their own Publications, or any other Catholic Book published in the United States, on receipt of the Retail price. This arrangement enables those who reside at the most distant part of the country to obtain Books at the same price as those who reside in the large cities. Persons need not pay more than the Catalogue price. Remit the money, and the Books will be promptly forwarded free of any further cost.

They promise particular care in enveloping and directing Books ordered to be sent by Mail, but will not be responsible for their safe arrival, as that depends wholly upon the Post-office authorities.

ANY BOOK, no matter where published, if to be had, can be pro cured and furnished at the lowest price by KELLY, PIET & Co.

PERSONS BUYING IN QUANTITIES, who desire their Goods Insured, are requested to give notice when ordering, as all Goods are shipped at the risk of the purchaser.

PARTICULAR ATTENTION given to the furnishing of Schools, Colleges, and Libraries with all Foreign or American Publications. Stationery, School Requisites, &c.

THE PACKING AND SHIPPING of Goods for distant points, by the cheapest and most reliable routes, receives their special care.

CLERGYMEN, SCHOOLS, RELIGIOUS INSTITUTIONS, Sunday School Libraries, and others buying in quantities, are allowed a *Liberal Discount*.

CATALOGUE
OF
KELLY, PIET & COMPANY,
PRINTERS,
PUBLISHERS, BOOKSELLERS & STATIONERS,
174 West Baltimore Street,

M. J. KELLY,
JNO. B. PIET,
T. J. KELLY,
W. F. POLLARD

BALTIMORE.

MARCH, 1870.

SCHOOL AND COLLEGE TEXT-BOOKS.

Catechisms, Irving's Series of.
Revised by M. J. Kerney.
Catechism of Astronomy.
Catechism of Botany.
Catechism Class'l, Biography.
Catechism of Chemistry.
Catechism of Grecian History.
Catechism of Grecian Antiquities.
Catechism Hist. of England.
Catechism of History of U. S.
Catechism Jewish Antiquities.
Catechism of Mythology.
Catechism Roman Antiquities.
Catechism of Roman History.
Catechism of Sacred History.
     Price 20c. each.

Creery, Wm. R.
Illustrated Primary School Spelling Book.................. 35
Key to the Exercises in Arithmetic contained in the Primary School Spelling Book. 50
Grammar School Spelling Book 50
Catechism of United States History 50

De Gournay, P. F.
First Steps in French, being an Introduction to the Study of the French Language........... 60

History of France,
For Schools. New edition, illustrated. 1 vol. 12mo. 416 pages.........:...... .... 1 75

Historiæ Sacræ.
Epitome Auctore, L'homond, editio *Nova Prosodiæ*, signis vocumque interpretatione adornata............................... 50

La Fontaine.
Fables Choisies, Nouvelle edition 75

Manual of Church History.
(For Schools.).................. 1 00

Maryland Series of Readers.
By Prof. M. A. Newell, Principal of the State Normal School, and Prof. Wm. R. Creery, Superintendent of Public Schools in Balto. city.
First Reader....... 25
Second Reader. 50
Third Reader...................... 75
Fourth Reader..................... 90
Fifth Reader....................... 1 25
Sixth Reader...................... 1 50

Ovid—Part One.
Ovidii Nasonis Selecta Fabulæ, ex Libris Metamorphoseon Publii. Notis illustratæ. Accedunt Quædam ex Libris Tristium Elegiæ. Pars Prima..... 60

Publications of Kelly, Piet & Co.

Ovid—Part Two.
Ovidii Nasonis Excerta Ex Libris Fastorum, Ex Tristium et Ex de Ponto, cum interpretatione et notis in usum scholarum digestis. Pars Secunda.. 75

Phædrus.
Phædri Augusti Liberti Fabularum Æsopiarum, Libri Quinque.. 50

Pizarro, Jose A.
Spanish Dialogues and English Conversations; adapted to the use of Spanish classes in schools and academies. 12mo. 1 00

Spanish Spelling and Reading Books.
Silabario Castellano, para el Uso de los Ninos. 18mo, paper............................... 20
Silabario Castellano, para el Uso de las Ninas. 18mo, paper................................. 20

Smith, Gen. F. H., (Virginia Military Institute.)
Elements of Geometry, by A. M. Legendere. With additions and modifications by M. A. Blanchet, Eleve of the Polytechnic School; Director of Studies at St. Barbe. Translated from the eleventh French edition. 1 vol. 8vo..................... 2 25

Elements of Trigonometry. Plain and Spherical. From the French of Lefebure de Fourcy, with Tables of Logarithms, of Numbers and of Sines and Cosines, and other Useful Tables. 1 vol. 8vo. 2 50

Smith, (Continued.)
Elements of Descriptive Geometry. With its applications to Shades, Shadows and Perspective, and Topography. Part I. 8vo.. 1 75

Tower, David B. (Revised Series.)
Algebra... 60
Key to ditto....................................... 60
Elements of Grammar..................... 40
Common School Grammar.......... 75
Gradual Lessons in Grammar...... 90
Grammar of Composition............. 75
First Reader....................................... 25
Second Reader................................ 45
Third Reader.................................... 60
Fourth Reader.................................. 75
Fifth Reader................................... 1 00
Sixth Reader.................................. 1 25
Gradual Speller................................ 25
Exercises in Articulation............... 20

Viris Illustribus Urbis Romæ.
A Romulo ad Augustum, Auctore L'homond, in Universitate, Parisiensi Professore Emerito.. 75

Wilson, Samuel F.
History of the American Revolution. With questions. 12mo. half roan...................................... 1 50

Williams and Packard's System of Penmanship.
Comprised in ten regularly graded Copy-books, and four intermediates............................... 20
The great simplicity and directness of its principles make it eminently adapted to class instruction. Instead of *parts of letters* being used as principals, together with "dots," "diminutive turns," and "exceptional forms," the whole system is comprised in five marks, viz: four curves and one straight line. Any intelligent teacher can, in two hours' time, place this scheme so plainly before a class, of whatever dimensions, that almost every member will be able to pass a close examination.

Weekly Report Books for use of Academies & Schools. p.doz.$1 25

FRENCH---Paris Editions.

Boileau. Œuvres Poetiques. With notes. 1 vol. 12mo. Half bound.................................. 1 75

Corneille. Theatre Œuvres Completes, avec notes et Commentaires. 2 vols., 12mo. Half bound 3 50

Publications of *Kelly, Piet & Co.* 5

Fleury, M. Lame.
Histoire Ancienne. 32mo.... $1 00
Histoire Grecque. 32mo...... 1 00
Histoire Moderne. 32mo...... 1 00
Histoire du Nouveau Testament. 32mo................ 1 00
Histoire Romaine, la Republique. 32mo......,...... 1 00
L'Histoire Romaine, l'Empire. 32mo 1 00
Histoire Sainte. 32mo.......... 1 00

Gaultier.
Lectures Graduees pour les Enfants du Premier age. Illustree. 2 vols., half bound...... 1 75
Leçons de Geographie. 32mo. 1 00

L'homond.
Elements de la Grammaire Française..........'........... 30

La Sage.
Histoire de Gil Blas de Santillane. 12mo, half bound..... 1 75

Madame de Stael.
Corinne, ou L'Italie. 1 vol., 12mo, half bound............ 1 75
L'Allemagne, (Germany.) 1 vol., 12mo, half bound......... 1 75

Madame de Sevigne.
Lettres Completes. With notes. 1 vol., 12mo, half bound...... 1 75

Moliere.
Œuvres Completes. With notes. 2 vols., 12mo, half bound............................ 3 50

Noel.
Gradus ad Parnassum, ou Nouveau Dictionnaire Poetique —Latin—Francaise............ 5 00

Racine.
Theatre Œuvres Completes. 12mo, half bound............... 1 75

MISCELLANEOUS BOOKS.

American Cyclops, (General B. F. Butler,) the Hero of New Orleans and Spoiler of Silver Spoons. Dubbed LL.D. By Pasquino. Embellished with Twelve Characteristic Etchings on copper. Demy, 4to, cloth extra, beveled boards... 1 50

Boyce, Rev. John.
Mary Lee; or, The Yankee in Ireland. 1 vol. 12mo. Illus... 1 50
Cloth extra, full gilt........... 2 00
The Spæwife; or, The Queen's Secret. 1 vol., 12mo, illustrated 2 00

Conscience, Hendrick.
The Lion of Flanders; or, The Battle of the Golden Spurs. 1 vol., 12mo, cloth............. 1 00
Cloth extra, full gilt........... 1 50

Dying Woodcutter,
The Goldsmith Artist, and Henrietta of England. 1 vol. Small 4to. Illustrated. Cloth, extra................................. 40

Danger of Ignorance;
The Cardinal's Dinner, and other Tales. 1 vol., small 4to. Illustrated. Cloth extra........ 40

Edgeworth, Maria.
Early Lessons, illustrated. 1 vol., 12mo, cloth, bev'd boards 1 50
Moral Tales. 1 vol., 12mo, cloth, illustrated.................. 1 50
Parent's Assistant. 1 vol., 12mo, cloth, illustrated.................. 1 50
Popular Tales. 1 vol., 12mo, cloth, illustrated.................. 1 50
Rosamond; A book for girls. 1 vol., 12mo, cloth, illustrated. 1 50

THE EDGEWORTH LIBRARY.
(Put up in Handsome Boxes.)
Frank............. 2 vols.
Harry and Lucy. 2 vols. } per set, 7 50
Rosamond. 1 vol.

THE HOME LIBRARY.
(Put up in Handsome Boxes.)
Early Lessons...............
Moral Tales..................
Parent's Assistant......... } per set, $6 00
Popular Tales...............

Publications of Kelly, Piet & Co.

Enchanted Keys, The,
and other Oriental Tales. 1 vol., 12mo, with illustrations. ... 1 50

Golden Pheasant,
Young Franklin, and Vanity Corrected. 1 vol., small 4to. Illustrated. Cloth extra....... 40

Howard, Frank Key.
Fourteen Months in American Bastiles. 1 vol., 8vo, paper. 25

Howard, T. E.
Excelsior; or, Essays on Politeness, Education, and the Means of Obtaining Success in Life 1 50

Lily of the Valley, The; or Margie and I, and other poems, by Amy Gray. 1 vol., 12mo. Bound in English cloth, beveled boards, ornamental side stamp...................... 1 50

Lucas, Daniel B.
The Wreath of Eglantine, and other poems. Illustrated, 1 vol. 12mo. Printed on tinted paper, bound in the best English cloth, with ornamental side stamp..................... 2 00

Moorman, Dr. J. J.
The Mineral Waters of the United States and Canada, with maps. 1 vol., 12mo, cloth 2 50

McSherry, Dr. Richard.
Early History of Maryland, and other Essays. 1 vol., 8vo, cloth............................ 1 25

PATRANAS LIBRARY,
Being Spanish stories, Legendary and Traditional, by the author of "Traditions of Tirol." Comprising—
The Irish Princess, and other Legendary Tales.
Dona Josefa, and other Popular Tales.
Carlo Magno and the Giant, and other Traditional and Legendary Tales.
The Black Charger of Hernando, and other Legendary Tales.
4 vols., square quarto. Each vol. illustrated. Price per set 2 00

Preston, Mrs. Margaret J.
Beechenbrook. A Rhyme of the War, and other Poems. An entirely new edition, with additions. Beautifully illustrated from designs by Wm. L. Sheppard, of Richmond, Va.

Small 4to Edition.
1 Turkey mor. antique, full gilt. 6 00
2 Turkey morocco, antique....... 5 00
3 Cloth extra, full gilt............. 3 50
Rockbridge Edition, with Frontispiece. 1 vol., 12mo, cloth. With ornamental side stamp.. 1 50
People's Edition. 12mo. Eighth thousand.
1 Cloth extra, gilt edge............ 1 50
2 Cloth extra....................... 1 00

Queen of Italy,
And other Tales. 1 vol., small 4to. Cloth extra.............. 40

Smith, Prof. Nathan R.
Fractures of the Lower Extremity, and the use of the Anterior Suspensory Apparatus in the treatment of those injuries. Fully illustrated by cuts and diagrams. 1 vol., 8vo, cloth........................... 3 00

The Golden Pheasant Library.
4 vols., small quarto, cloth, full gilt backs. Each volume illustrated, and each set put up in a neat box. Comprising—
The Golden Pheasant.
The Dying Woodcutter, and other tales.
The Queen of Italy, and other tales.
The Danger of Ignorance, and other tales.
Price per set, 1 60

Wilson, Samuel F.
History of the American Revolution, with a preliminary view of the character and principles of the Colonists. 1 vol., 12mo. Illustrated 1 50

Publications of Kelly, Piet & Co. 7

CATHOLIC PRAYER BOOKS.

Little Crown of Jesus, The.
A Manual of Devotions and other Instructions most frequently required. Published with the approbation of the Most Rev. M. J. SPALDING, Archbishop of Baltimore.

1 Cloth, gilt back...............	40
2 Cloth, full gilt edges & sides..	75
3 Embossed mor., plain edge..	60
4 Embossed mor., gilt edge....	75
5 Embossed mor., gilt edge, and clasp.................	90
6 Levant morocco, red edge...	1 00
7 American mor., full gilt......	1 00
8 Amer. mor., full gilt & clasp,	1 25
9 Morocco tucks, gilt edge......	1 00
10 Turkey morocco case..........	1 50
11 Turkey morocco, and clasp..	1 75
12 Turkey morocco, super extra	2 00
13 Turkey mor., extra & clasp...	2 50
14 English calf, red edges........	2 25
15 Turkey mor., ex. rims & clasp	4 00

Christian's Guide to Heaven, The. A Manual of Spiritual Exercises for Catholics, with the Evening Office of the Church, in Latin and English, the Epistles and Gospels for all Sundays and Holydays, and a Selection of Pious Hymns. Corrected, enlarged and published with the approbation of the Most Rev. Archbishop of Baltimore. 32mo.

1 Cloth, plain..................	50
1½ Cloth extra, full gilt............	75
2 Arabesque, plain.................	60
3 Arabesque, gilt edge..............	90
4 Roan, full gilt.....................	1 00
5 Roan, full gilt and clasp........	1 25
6 American mor., full gilt........	1 25
7 Amer. mor., full gilt and clasp	1 50
8 Turkey morocco, super extra..	2 25
9 Turkey, super extra and clasp	2 75
10 Eng. calf extra, red or gilt edge	2 50
11 Turkey morocco extra, beveled and paneled...............	4 00
12 Turkey morocco extra, rims and clasp.....................	4 50
13 Velvet extra, full mounted...	8 00
14 Velvet extra, heavy octagon rims, clasp and side ornaments.............................	9 00

Child's Daily Prayer Book.
This little book has been prepared for the use of Catholic Children, and contains Morning and Evening Prayers, short prayers at Mass, and is *illustrated by thirty-six full-page engravings of the Mass,* with instructions and directions for Confession, Communion and Confirmation. Published with the approbation of the Most Rev. M. J. SPALDING, Archbishop of Baltimore. It is, without exception, *the best prayer book for children ever issued.*

1 Cloth............................		25
2 Cloth, full gilt sides and edge		40
3 Arabesque, plain...............		40
4 Arabesque, gilt edges..........		60
5 American morocco, full gilt,		75
6 American morocco tuck......		75
7 Levant morocco...............		75
8 Turkey morocco, super extra	1	25
9 Turkey, super ext. and clasp,	1	50
10 English calf, extra red edge..	2	00

Flowers of Devotion, compiled from approved sources. Published with the approbation of the Most Rev. M. J. SPALDING, D. D., Archbishop of Baltimore. 1 vol., 48mo.

1 Cloth, gilt backs..............		30
2 Cloth, full gilt sides & edges,		50
3 Embossed mor., plain edge...		45
4 Embossed mor., gilt edge.....		60
5 Levant morocco, red edge...		75
6 American morocco, full gilt,		75
7 Amer mor., full gilt & clasp,	1	00
8 Turkey mor., super extra.....	1	50
9 Turkey mor., sup. ex. & clasp	2	00
10 English calf extra, red edges	2	00
11 Turkey mor., ex. rims & clasp	3	50
12 Morocco tuck, gilt edge.......		75

The Little Companion of the Sisters of Mercy. A Manual of Daily Devotions for the use of the Sisters of Mercy, to which is added Officium Parvum Beatæ Mariæ Virginis. 32mo.

1 Arabesque, plain......		75
2 Arabesque, gilt edge...........	1	00

Publications of Kelly, Piet & Co.

The Ursuline Manual; a Collection of Prayers, Spiritual Exercises, &c. Originally arranged for the young ladies educated at the Ursuline Convent, Cork. *Revised and improved by Bishop England* for the use of the young ladies educated at the Ursuline Convent, Charleston, South Carolina.

1 Cloth, extra...............................$	75
2 Arabesque, plain edge...........	1 00
3 Arabesque, gilt edge.............	1 25
4 Arabesque, gilt edge & clasp..	1 50
5 American morocco, full gilt..	1 50
6 American morocco and clasp	2 00
7 Turkey morocco, full gilt....	2 50
8 Turkey morocco and clasp...	3 00
9 Turkey, super extra............	3 00
10 Turkey, super extra & clasp..	3 50
11 English calf extra, red edge..	3 50
12 Turkey morocco extra, beveled and paneled...............	4 50
13 Velvet extra, full mounted and clasp...........................	10 00
14 Velvet extra, full mounted, ornamented sides...............	12 00
15 Turkey morocco, extra rims and clasp...........................	5 00

Office of Holy Week; *in Latin and English—large type*, with the ordinary Rubrics, Summary of the Psalms, Explanations of the Ceremonies and Mysteries; together with observations and devout reflections. Translated from the Italian of Alexander Mazzinelli. Published with the approbation of the Most Rev. Archbishop of Baltimore.

1 Cloth, extra........................	75
2 Arabesque, plain edge.........	1 00
3 Arabesque, gilt edge...........	1 25
4 American morocco, full gilt.	2 00
5 Turkey morocco, extra........	3 00
6 English calf, extra..............	3 50

This new edition has been very carefully revised. The Office for Easter Sunday, the Ordinary of the Mass, and the Order of Blessing Holy Oils have been added, making it the most complete edition ever published.

The Catholic's Vade Mecum; A Pocket Manual of Prayers for Daily Use.

It can readily be carried in the pocket, the size being five by three inches, and may be justly considered the most perfect Prayer Book for its size published in the United States. Containing all the usual Devotions for daily use; four different Forms of Mass Prayers, including Mass for the Dead; the authorized copy of the Litany of the Holy Name, and a large number of other Litanies; the Devotions for the Forty Hours; Way of the Cross, *with illustrations;* Vespers for the Sundays and different Festivals of the year; a great variety of Prayers before and after Communion, &c.

For a pious Catholic a small Prayer Book is an almost indispensable companion, provided it contains a selection of those devotions which are most frequently required.

1 Embossed, cloth...................$	75
2 Arabesque, plain................	1 00
3 Arabesque, gilt edge...........	1 25
4 Arabesque, gilt edge & clasp,	1 50
5 Levant morocco, red edge...	1 25
6 American morocco, full gilt,	1 50
7 Amer. mor., full gilt & clasp,	1 75
8 Turkey morocco case...........	2 25
8½ Turkey mor., case and clasp	2 75
9 Turkey morocco, tuck.........	2 00
10 Turkey, super extra............	3 00
11 Turkey, super extra & clasp..	3 50
12 Super English calf, red edges	3 50
13 Turkey mor., paneled sides..	4 50
14 Turkey mor., extra rims and clasp...........................	5 00
15 Velvet, full mounted & clasp,	10 00
16 Velvet extra, heavy octagon rims and clasps, side ornaments..............................	12 00

Key of Heaven. (With Epistles and Gospels.) 24mo. Revised and improved, forming one of the very best prayer books in the language. Published with the approbation of the Most Rev. M. J. SPALDING, Archbishop of Baltimore.

1 Cloth...................................	50
1½ Cloth extra, full gilt...........	90
2 Arabesque, plain................	75
3 Arabesque, gilt...................	90
4 Arabesque, gilt and clasp....	1 25
5 Levant, morocco, red edge...	1 25
6 American morocco, full gilt.	1 50
7 American mor. and clasp....	1 75
8 Turkey, super ex., gilt edge,	2 50
9 Turkey, super extra & clasp.:	3 00
10 English calf, extra..............	3 50
11 Turkey mor., ex. rims & clasp	5 00

Mission Book, The. (Compiled by the Redemptorist Fathers.)
A Manual of Instruction and Prayers, adapted to preserve the Fruits of the Mission. Drawn chiefly from the works of St. Alphonsus Liguori. Compiled by the Fathers of the Congregation of the Most Holy Redeemer, *and used at all their Missions* throughout the United States. Published with the approbation of the Most Rev. M. J. SPALDING, Archbishop of Baltimore.

1 Cloth, extra........................	75	7 Turkey morocco, full gilt....	2 50
2 Arabesque, plain................	1 00	8 Turkey morocco and clasp...	3 00
3 Arabesque, gilt edges..........	1 25	9 Turkey, super extra............	3 00
4 Arabesque, gilt edges and clasp.............................	1 50	10 Turkey, super extra and clasp..............................	3 50
5 American morocco, full gilt,	1 50	11 English calf extra, red edges,	3 50
6 American morocco, full gilt, and clasp........................	2 00	12 Turkey mor. extra rims and clasp.............................	5 00

CATECHISMS.

A General Catechism of the Christian Doctrine, *prepared by order of the First Plenary Council of Baltimore,* for the use of the Catholics in the United States of America. Published with the approbation of the Most Rev. M. J. SPALDING, D. D., Archbishop of Baltimore. 32mo., 84 pages, printed from LARGE TYPE, and bound in paper covers...5c. each Per 100, *Net,* $2 75.

This edition is printed in LARGER TYPE than any heretofore published, and is consequently the most popular Catechism of Christian Doctrine in the market.

An Abridged Catechism of *the First Plenary Council of Baltimore,* for persons who may not be able to learn the larger one. Published with the approbation of the Most Rev. M. J. SPALDING, D. D., Archbishop of Baltimore. 32mo, paper covers...........3c. each Per 100, *Net,* $1 75.

Catechism of Perseverance.
An Historical, Doctrinal, Moral and Liturgical Exposition of the Catholic Religion. Translated from the French of Abbe Gaume. By Rev. F. B. Jamison 75

MUSIC BOOKS.

A MANUAL OF ROMAN CHANT. Compiled from authentic sources, for the use of Churches, Seminaries, and Religious Communities. By a Priest of the Congregation of the Most Holy Redeemer.
1 vol., 4to. 232 pages, neatly bound in Cloth................................ $1 75

THE VESPER-PSALTER; or, Psalmody Made Easy. Comprising all the Vesper Psalms, with the Canticle, Magnificat, set in Modern Notation to the Roman Psalm-Tones, with easy Organ Accompaniments. By a Priest of the Congregation of the Most Holy Redeemer. With the approbation of the Most Reverend Archbishop of Baltimore.
1 vol., 4to 3 50

THE LITTLE VESPER BOOK. A Supplement to the Manual of Roman Chant. 12mo. Cloth... 75

STANDARD CATHOLIC BOOKS.

Anderdon, Rev. W. H.
Antoine de Bonneval, a tale of Paris in the days of St. Vincent de Paul. 1 vol., 12mo.
Illustrated. Cloth beveled... $1 50
Cloth, extra full gilt............ 2 00

Adelmar, The Templar,
A Tale of the Crusades. Translated from the French. 1 vol., 18mo. Cloth................ 40
Cloth, extra, full gilt............ 60

Aurelia.
Aurelia, or the Jews of Capena Gate. Translated from the French. 1 vol. Illustrated. 12mo. Cloth, beveled......... 1 50
Cloth, extra full gilt............ 2 00

Banquet of Theodulus;
Or, Reunion of the different Christian Communions. By the late Baron de Starck. 12mo. Cloth 1 00

Blanche,
A Tale translated from the French. 1 vol., 18mo. Cloth, 40
Cloth extra, full gilt............ 60

Catechism of Vows.
For the use of Persons Consecrated to God in the Religious State. By Rev. Father Peter Cotel, S. J. Translated from the French. 1 vol., 18mo. Cloth extra 50

Challoner, Rt. Rev. Bishop.
Catholic Christian Instructed in the Sacraments, Sacrifice, and Ceremonies of the Church.
Flexible cloth..................... 25
Cloth extra........................ 50

Christmas Night's Entertainments; or, The Pastor's Visit to the Science of Salvation. Translated from the Spanish. 18mo, cloth extra................ 75
Cloth extra, full gilt............ 1 00

Ceremonial,
For the use of the Catholic Churches in the United States. Originally published by order of the first Council of Baltimore, with the approbation of the Holy See. Third edition, carefully revised and considerably enlarged and illustrated with numerous engravings. 1 vol., 12mo.
Cloth extra, beveled............ 3 00
Cloth extra, full gilt............ 3 75

Ceremonial,
For the Reception and Profession of the Religious Sisters of Mercy. 1 vol., 8vo. Beautifully printed in Red and Black. Net..................... 75

Dalgairns, Rev. J. B.
Devotion to the Heart of Jesus. With an introduction to the History of Jansenism. By Rev. J. B. Dalgairns. 18mo.
Cloth extra........................ 75
Cloth extra, full gilt............ 1 00

Devotions to the Holy Guardian Angels, in the form of Considerations, Prayers, Pious Practices and Examples. Translated from the Italian of Rev. P. De Mattei, S.J. 32mo. Cloth................................ 50

Double Sacrifice, The;
Or, The Pontifical Zouaves. A Tale of Castlefidardo. Translated from the Flemish. Cloth, extra beveled, illustrated 1 50
Cloth extra, full gilt............ 2 00

Dupanloup, Bishop of Orleans. The Future Œcumenical Council; a letter of the Bishop of Orleans to the clergy of his Diocese. 1 vol., 8vo, paper.............................. 25

Epistles and Gospels for all the Sundays and Principal Festivals throughout the Year. 1 vol., 32mo. Cloth extra... 25

Publications of Kelly, Piet & Co. 11

Eudoxia;
A Picture of the Fifth Century, freely translated from the German of Ida, Countess of Hahn-Hahn. 1 vol., 12mo. Cloth extra, beveled.................. 1 50
Cloth extra, full gilt............ 2 00

Excerpta ex Rituali Romano. Pro administratione Sacramentorum, ad commodiorem usum Missionariorum, in Septentrionalis Americæ Fœderatæ Provinciis. Editio Sexta, 1869. (The Prayers and Passages for the Administration of the Sacraments have been added in English, French, and German. 32mo.
1 Arabesque, plain............... 75
2 Arabesque, gilt edges........ 1 00
3 Turkey, super extra.......... 2 00
4 Turkey, super extra, ribbon edge or tuck................... 2 50
5 English calf, extra............. 2 50

Encyclical Letter of Pope Pius IX., given at St. Peter's, Rome, Dec. 8, 1864, together with the Syllabus of Errors Condemned. Third edition....... 25

Eva Fitzgerald;
Or, Scenes in Erin and the Sister Isle. 1 vol., 18mo. Cloth, extra................................. 50
Cloth extra, full gilt 75

Father Larkin's Mission.
A Tale of the Times. By Dr. T. L. Nichols. 18mo. Cloth, 40
Cloth extra, full gilt............ 60

Furniss, Rev. J., C. S. S. R.
Tracts for Spiritual Reading, designed for First Communions, Retreats, Missions, &c. 1 vol., 12mo, cloth........ 1 00

Fullerton, Lady Georgiana.
Laurentia; a Tale of Japan in the Sixteenth Century. 12mo. Cloth extra, beveled............ 1 25
Cloth extra, full gilt............ 1 75

Gerald O'Reilly;
Or, The Triumph of Principle, together with Eva O'Beirne; or, The Little Lace Maker. Two Tales, by Brother James. 1 vol., 18mo. Cloth, extra... 50
Cloth extra, full gilt............ 75

Ghost, The.
A Comedy in Three Acts. Taken from the French. 1 vol. 50

Grace O'Halloran;
Or, Ireland and its Peasantry. A tale of the day. By Agnes M. Stewart. 1 vol., 18mo. Cloth....................................... 60
Cloth extra, full gilt............ 75

Herbert, (Lady.) The Mission of St. Francis de Sales in the Chablais. Cloth extra, full gilt 2 50

Hay, Rt. Rev. Dr. George.
The Devout Christian instructed in the Faith of Christ, from the written word. 1 vol., 12mo, cloth......................... 1 25

Hearn, Rev. J. A.
Reflections on the Passion of our Divine Lord, in Verse. 12mo. Cloth.......................... 75

Hortense;
Or, Pride Corrected. A tale of true generosity and goodness. 18mo. Cloth extra... 40
Cloth, full gilt.................... 60

Isle of the Dead;
Or, The Keeper of the Lazaretto. From the French of Emile Souvestre. 18mo. Cloth................................. 40
Cloth extra, full gilt............ 60

Joy of the Christian Soul.
Translated from the French of Pere Lombez. By Rev. E. Damphoux. 18mo, cloth...... 40

Justice and Mercy;
Or, a Tale of All Hallow E'en. By Miss A. M. Stewart, author of "The World and the Cloister," "Gertrude," "Grace O'Halloran," &c., &c. A neat 18mo. volume. Cloth... 60
Cloth extra, full gilt............ 75

Jubilee Manual.
A Manual of Instructions on the Jubilee and Prayers recommended to be said in the Station Churches. Published by the authority of the Most Rev. Archbishop of Baltimore. 32mo, paper. Single copies... 3
Per 100, $1.50. Per 1,000, $12.

Kenrick, Most Rev. F. P.,
Archbishop of Baltimore. A
Revised Version of the Bible.
Translated from the Latin
Vulgate, diligently compared
with the original text. Being
a revised edition of the Douay
version, with notes, critical
and explanatory. In five octavo volumes. Cloth extra.... 20 00
Half Turkey, antique............... 30 00
Full Turkey extra, antique........ 60 00
Full Turkey extra, paneled sides 75 00
The separate volumes will be
supplied at the following prices:

The Pentateuch;
Or, The Five Books of Moses.
Cloth... 3 50
Library style, marble edges.. 4 00

The Historical Books.
Cloth extra............................... 4 00
Library style, marble edges... 4 50

New Testament.
Cloth... 3 50
Library style, marble edges... 4 50
Half Turkey, antique............... 5 00
Full Turkey, antique................ 9 00
Full Turkey, antique, paneled
sides... 12 00

**Lacordaire's Letters to Young
Men.** Edited by the Count de
Montalembert. Translated by
Rev. James Trenor. 1 vol.,
12mo, cloth extra, beveled.... 1 50
Cloth extra, full gilt................ 2 00

Law and Wilberforce's Letters to their Parishioners, giving their reasons for submitting to the Catholic Church.
Paper 30

Life of St. Stanislaus Kostka,
Of the Society of Jesus.
Patron of Movices. 1 vol.
18mo. Cloth extra.................... 60
Cloth extra, full gilt................ 75

Life of the Very Rev. Felix
de Andreis, First Superior of
the Congregation of the Mission in the United States, and
Vicar-General of the Diocese
of New Orleans. With portrait. 1 vol., 12mo, cloth.... 1 50

Life of the Cure D'Ars,
(Rev. J. B. M. Vianney,) the
celebrated Parish Priest of Ars,
France, who died in the odor
of sanctity, August 4, 1859.
By the Abbe Alfred Monin.
Abridged from the French by
Rev. B. S. Piot. 1 vol.,18mo. 75
Cloth extra, full gilt............... 1 25

Life of John Mary Decalogne,
a Student of the University of
Paris. Translated from the
French. 1 vol., 18mo., embellished with a neat and appropriate frontispiece. Cloth, 60
Cloth, extra full gilt.............. 1 00

Life of St. Louis, King of
France. Translated from the
French. 1 vol., 18mo., cloth, 40
Cloth, extra full gilt.............. 60

Little Month of St. Joseph.
Containing Prayers, Meditations and an Example for each
day for the month of March.
32mo. Cloth........................... 40
Cloth, flexible......................... 25

Life in the Cloister;
Or, Faithful and True. By
Agnes M. Stewart. 12mo.
Cloth extra, beveled.............. 1 25
Cloth extra, full gilt.............. 1 75

Lionello,
A sequel to the Jew of Verona.
By Rev. A. Breciani, S. J.
Embellished with a characteristic frontispiece. 12mo. Cloth
extra, beveled......................... 1 50
Cloth extra, full gilt.............. 2 00

Little Testament of our Lord
Jesus Christ, or an Admonition, Aspiration and Practice
for each day............................ 15

Manning, Most Rev. H. E.
Grounds of Faith. Four Lectures delivered in St. George's
Church, Southwark. 18mo.
Cloth.. 40
Paper 15

Publications of Kelly, Piet & Co. 13

Manual of Piety,
For the use Seminaries. 32mo.
Roan, embossed 75
Roan, embossed gilt 1 00
Turkey, super extra 2 00

Massingers, The;
Or, The Evils of Mixed Marriages. Dedicated, by permission, to his Eminence Cardinal Wiseman. 12mo.
Cloth extra, beveled 1 25
Cloth extra, full gilt 1 75

McGill, Rt. Rev. John, D.D.
Our Faith the Victory; or, a comprehensive view of the Principal Doctrines of the Christian Religion. 1 vol., demy, 8vo., cloth, extra 2 00
Half Turkey, morocco antique 3 50

Meditations and Considerations, for a Retreat of one day in each month. Compiled from the Writings of the Society of Jesus. 1 vol., 18mo.
Cloth 60
Cloth extra, full gilt 75

Miles, Geo. H.
The Governess; or, The Effects of Good Example. Being a leaf from every-day life. An original tale. 18mo.
Cloth extra 75
Cloth extra, full gilt 1 00

Loretto; or, The Choice. A story written for the old, and for the young. In four parts.
Cloth extra, beveled boards... 1 25
Cloth extra, full gilt 1 75

Muller, Rev. Michael, C.SS.R.
Blessed Eucharist, our Greatest Treasure. 1 vol., 12mo.
cloth, extra beveled 1 50
Cloth extra, full gilt 3 00

Prayer, the Key of Salvation.
1 vol. 12mo, cloth, beveled. 1 50
Cloth extra, full gilt 2 00

Office of the Blessed Virgin
Mary (in Latin) for the Three Seasons of the Year, with the Penitential Psalms, the Litany of the Saints, the Office of the Dead, &c., according to the Roman Breviary. Reprinted from the last Mechlin Edition. 18mo., cloth 75

Panegyric of the Blessed
Aloysius. By Rev. Dr. O'Connell, of St. Mary's, Oscott. 18mo, cloth 25

Poor Man's Catechism;
Or, The Christian Doctrine Explained. With short admonitions. By Rev. John Mannock, O. S. B. 1 vol., 12mo.
Flexible cloth 25
Cloth, extra 50

Protesting Christian Standing Before the Judgment Seat of Christ, to answer for his Protest against the Parent Church. By Rev. J. Perry.
Paper 12
Cloth, flexible 20

Pious Exercises and Practices in honor of the Sacred Heart of Mary. 32mo, paper, 15

Piot, Rev. B. S.
Glimpses of Heaven. Translated from the French of St. F. de Sales and Father Lambillotte. 32mo 20

Roman Martyrology, The.
Published by order of Gregory XIII; revised by the authority of Urban VIII and Clement X; afterwards, in the year 1749, augmented and corrected by Benedict XIV. Last edition according to the copy printed at Rome in 1845. 1 vol., 12mo, crimson cloth, *Net,* 3 00

Ritus et Preces ad Missam
Celebrandam in unum præcipue eorem qui sacris initiantur. 32mo. Roan 75
Roan, gilt 1 00
Turkey, super extra 2 00

Soul on Calvary Meditating on the Sufferings of Jesus Christ, and finding at the foot of the Cross consolation in her troubles; with prayers, practices, and examples on various subjects. 1 vol., 18mo. Cloth, ... 75

Sermons Delivered in the Cathedral during the Second Plenary Council of Baltimore with an interesting account of the Public Sessions of the Council. Embellished with a Photograph Group of Archbishops Spalding, Purcell, Odin, McCloskey, and Blanchett, together with two fine Engravings of the Procession and Council in Session. 1 vol., 12mo. Cloth, beveled.................................... 3 00
Half calf, extra..................... 3 75

The Month of Mary Conceived Without Sin. Translated from the French of Rev. A. Gratry, Priest of the Oratory of the Immaculate Conception. With an Introduction by the Very Rev. F. W. Faber. D. D. 18mo. Cloth, 50
Cloth, full gilt..................... 75

The Way of the Cross; or, The Fourteen Stations of the Cross, from the Raccolta, and as practised in the Cathedral of Baltimore. Paper........... 10

The Studies and Teachings of the Society of Jesus, at the time of its suppression in 1750–73. Translated from the French of Abbe Maynard. 12mo, cloth extra............... 1 00

The Orphan Sisters; Or, Pupils of the Common School. A Drama for Girls, in One Act. By a Catholic Clergyman........................ 20

Theolinda and Adeline; Or, The Young Maiden and the Lute. A tale. 18mo, cloth, 40
Cloth extra, full gilt............. 60

Two Cottages, The. A tale showing how many more families may be made happy than are so. By Lady Georgianna Fullerton. 18mo. Cloth extra.......................... 50
Cloth extra, full gilt............ 75

Ullathorne, Rt. Rev. Bishop. Immaculate Conception of the Mother of God. An Exposition. 18mo, cloth............... 75

Vision of Old Andrew. The Vision of Old Andrew the Weaver. Embellished with a neat Frontispiece. 18mo. Cloth extra........................... 60
Cloth, full gilt, ... 75

Wiseman. H. E. Cardinal. The Hidden Gem. A Drama in Two Acts. Embellished with a portrait of the Author. (A new edition in press.)

Lectures on the Real Presence of the Body of our Lord Jesus Christ in the Blessed Eucharist. 12mo. Cloth............ 1 50

Lectures on the Offices and Ceremonies of Holy Week. With Ten Illustrations. 1 vol., 12mo. Cloth........................ 1 00

Lectures on the Principal Doctrines and Practices of the Catholic Church. 1 vol., 12mo. Cloth 2 00

Lamp of the Sanctuary, to which is added Mary, Model of Filial Piety. 1 vol., 18mo. Cloth, 40
Cloth extra, full gilt............ 75

White, Rev. C. I., D. D. The Mission and Duties of Young Women. Translated from the French. 1 vol., 18mo. 60
Cloth extra, full gilt............ 1 00

Wilberforce, Rev. J. An Inquiry into the Principles of Church Authority; or, Reasons for Recalling my Subscription to the Royal Supremacy. 12mo., cloth...................... 1 25

Publications of Kelly, Piet & Co. 15

Foreign Newspapers and Periodicals.

KELLY, PIET & CO.

Having been appointed the Agents for the following Periodicals, feel great gratification in being able to offer them to the Catholics of the United States at such low rates, and hope for a liberal encouragement.

THE WEEKLY (LONDON) REGISTER,

For $12 per year (including postage), United States currency. THE WEEKLY REGISTER AND CATHOLIC STANDARD, a First-class Family Newspaper. Established in 1849. THE WEEKLY REGISTER reports fully the Catholic and General News of the Week. Particular attention is devoted to Foreign and English Literature.

THE (LONDON) TABLET,

(The old established Catholic Paper.) $12 per year (including postage), United States currency. Published every Friday. THE TABLET has for twenty-six years been the advocate of the interests of the Catholic body. It has always maintained the expediency of the union of all Catholics in a strong and independent line of policy; is opposed to that of keeping the rights of the Catholics as British subjects in abeyance, to suit the views of political parties, who are thought by some to be less hostile to the concession of these rights than others. THE TABLET devotes considerable space to Reviews, and the Weekly Summary and Digest of Home and Foreign News is a marked feature in the paper.

THE WESTMINSTER GAZETTE,

For $7 per year (including postage), United States currency. Published every Saturday in London. The New Catholic Weekly Paper, THE WESTMINSTER GAZETTE, supported by a large number of known and approved writers, English and Foreign. Its two main objects are, first, the exposition of Catholic principles on all those great questions—ecclesiastical, philosophical, and social—which are now agitating the intellect and heart of the country; and, secondly, a truthful statement of facts as to the condition, political and religious, of Catholicism in the various countries of Europe. An important feature of the GAZETTE is the large space especially allotted to Reviews of Books, both English and Foreign, non-Catholic as well as Catholic.

THE MONTH,

A Magazine and Review. Edited by the Jesuit Fathers in London. Published on the first of each month. $5 per year, United States currency; single numbers, 50 cents. Subscriptions commence January and July. In order to increase the circulation of this interesting Monthly in the United States, we have made arrangements by which we can supply it at the low price of $5 per year, United States currency, in advance. It contains articles on Literature, Art, Science, Philosophy, History, and Theology, Reviews of Books, Original Fiction, and Poetry.

THE LAMP,

An Illustrated Monthly Journal of General Literature. Subscription, $3, United States currency.

THE DUBLIN (QUARTERLY) REVIEW,

For $10 per year, United States currency. This sterling Catholic Quarterly maintains the high character it has enjoyed so many years. Single Numbers, $3.

ETUDES RELIGIEUSES, HISTORIQUES ET LITTERAIRES.

Par les Peres de la Compagnie de Jesus. Published Monthly. $8 per year.

REVUE DES QUESTIONS HISTORIQUES.

(Quarterly.) $12 per year.

LE CONTEMPORAIN:

Revue d'Economie Chretienne. Litterature, Histoire, Philosophie, Science, Theologie, Beaux-Arts, Voyages, Economie Charitable, Bibliographie, etc. Published Monthly. $12 per year.

Subscriptions received for LE MONDE, L'UNIVERS, LE FRANCAIS, or any of the French Periodicals, prices for which will be furnished on

PERIODICALS

The Catholic Mirror,

OFFICIAL ORGAN

Of the Archbishop of Baltimore, and Bishops of Richmond, Wheeling, Wilmington, and Vicariate Apostolic of North Carolina.

A FIRST-CLASS FAMILY NEWSPAPER.
PUBLISHED EVERY SATURDAY.

Terms of Subscription, Per Annum, by Mail, $3.00.

ACTA EX IIS
DECERPTA
QUAE APUD SANCTAM SEDEM
GERUNTUR
IN COMPENDIUM OPPORTUNE REDACTA
ET ILLUSTRATA.

Published Monthly.
SUBSCRIPTION PRICE, $3.50 PER ANNUM, IN ADVANCE.

Approbation of the Most Reverend Archbishop.

We cordially recommend to the Very Reverend and Reverend Clergy of our Jurisdiction the republication of the valuable Roman Monthly, the "*Acta Ex Iis Decerpta Quae Apud Sanctam Sedem Geruntur*," undertaken, with our full approbation, by Messrs. Kelly, Piet & Co., of Baltimore.

M. J. SPALDING, *Archbishop of Baltimore.*

Baltimore, June 18th, 1869.

THE PRACTITIONER.
A Monthly Journal of Therapeutics.

Edited by FRANCIS E. ANSTIE, M. D., F. R. C. P., Senior Assistant Physician to Westminster Hospital. Terms of Subscription, Four Dollars per year, in advance. Single Copies, 40 Cents.

www.ingramcontent.com/pod-product-compliance
Lightning Source LLC
Chambersburg PA
CBHW020802230426
43666CB00007B/815